In the Beginning

by Laurie Polich

50

Devotions

for Teens

on Genesis

TWO MORE BY LAURIE POLICH

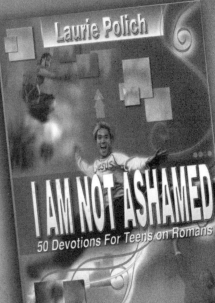

I AM NOT ASHAMED: 50 DEVOTIONS FOR TEENS ON ROMANS:

This resource brings the Book of Romans to the world of today's youth. Serving a double purpose—both as devotional and Bible commentary—this book helps youth connect their lives with Scripture. Questions for reflection are offered as well, making it easy for youth leaders to use it as a program resource.

ISBN: 0687081181

DIVE INTO LIVING WATER: 50 DEVOTIONS FOR TEENS ON THE GOSEPL OF JOHN:

These devotions take teens through the Book of John. Each two-page devotion covers 10–30 verses. Youth leaders find dozens of illustrations, questions for reflection, program ideas.

ISBN: 0687052238

DIMENSIONS FOR LIVING

cell. Yet that was the road that led him to Pharaoh's palace. Joseph was able to use his gifts to provide for the future of thousands of people. But it all came at the cost of personal pain.

While we don't always know the reasons *for* pain, we know that God has a purpose *in* it. The question is, does God really understand how it feels?

Those of us who live after Jesus know the answer to that question; it comes when we look to the cross. No matter how much we suffer, we'll never suffer more than Jesus did. And we have a God who has gone before us to carry us through.

1. Have you ever looked back on something bad that happened, and seen God's purpose in it? If so, did it change your perspective? Why, or why not?

...And there was light.

2. How important was it that Joseph was healed from his childhood wounds? Do you think that things would have turned out differently if Joseph hadn't been healed?

3. Have you ever experienced suffering? If so, how did it affect your relationship with God? How does Joseph's perspective in this chapter give us a different perspective on suffering?

In the Beginning

by Laurie Polich

50

Devotions

for Teens

on Genesis

DIMENSIONS
FOR LIVING

IN THE BEGINNING:
50 DEVOTIONS FOR TEENS ON GENESIS

COPYRIGHT © 2005 BY DIMENSIONS FOR LIVING

This book is printed on acid-free, recycled paper.

ISBN 0-687-73972-1

Cover Design: Keely Moore

05 06 07 08 09 10 11 12 13 14—10 9 8 7 6 5 4 3 2 1

MANUFACTURED IN THE UNITED STATES OF AMERICA

Contents

Dedication

To Vivian McIlraith:

May she have the courage to continue her journey,

as much as she's given me the courage to live mine.

Acknowledgments

Special thanks to:

Stacy Sharpe, Vicki Stairs, Marlo McCauley, Susie Peterson, and Teri Vogeli: Your friendship is priceless, and your love and support this last year helped carry me through.

John Cervenka: You are a rare and treasured friend. Thank you for your consistent care and presence in my life.

Melissa Johnston: I'm grateful that God brought you to Camp Pendleton and brought us together as friends.

The Mariners Small Group Bible Study: What a blessing to not only learn from Beth, but from each of you!

Thank you for sharing your lives.

Katie and Haley, Hudson and Truman Polich: You have brought

boundless joy into our family, and your arrival shows us all that the Journey continues on.

Introduction

Genesis is a book of stories. And these stories have the power to change our lives. While these stories are about certain people at a certain time, they carry messages for all people at all times. That's why they speak to you and me.

The word *Genesis* means "history of origin," and the Book of Genesis shows us where we began. From Adam to Noah, Abraham to Joseph, the genealogies of Genesis unfold the beginnings of human life. They also show us God's role in creating and orchestrating that life. But the miracle of Genesis is that the stories of these people speak to our own stories, and God's Word reaches beyond the pages of this book to transform us.

In the New Testament, spiritual truth is conveyed through lessons and parables; so we unpack verses and passages to illuminate their meaning. In Genesis, spiritual truth is conveyed through stories and events; so we let the stories speak for themselves. For that reason, each devotional will zero in on the details of the stories to maximize the impact of the story itself. My guess is that these stories will fascinate you. And they'll leave you thinking for some time to come.

At the top of each devotional, you'll find a portion of the Scripture from each chapter of Genesis. I recommend that you read the entire chapter in your Bible, rather than just the verses included in this book. Otherwise, it's a bit like reading the Cliff Notes®, instead of the actual book—you miss the depth and richness of the author's intent. And when the Author is God, that's a lot to miss!

On a personal note, this devotional was written at a time of intense personal and spiritual struggle. Perhaps that's what makes it so meaningful to me. While I hope and pray that these stories speak to your lives, the most powerful thing about writing this book was how they spoke to mine. God used it to reposition me in my journey of faith.

From Genesis, we learn that hope comes from struggle, perseverance comes from pain, and life is found in letting go. My prayer for you is that these stories will inspire you to live your own story well—not only for yourself, but for the part you will play in the grand story—God's story. That is why you are here.

–Laurie Polich

11

In the Beginning....

Genesis 1

Then God said, "Let us make humankind in our image, according to our likeness; and let them have dominion over the fish of the sea, and over the birds of the air, and over the cattle, and over all the wild animals of the earth, and over every creeping thing that creeps upon the earth."

And God said...

So God created humankind in his image, in the image of God he created them; male and female he created them.
(Genesis 1:26-27, NRSV)

In the beginning God ... .

The first four words of the Bible reveal an important truth: God was here before Creation began. So how did God get here? Has God always been here? Those questions aren't answered in the Bible. The answers are most likely beyond our human comprehension. We think in terms of beginnings and ends, but God exists outside of time, because God created time (see verse 5), so God has no beginning or end. For God, there is no past or future; so God can be everywhere at once.

Before your brain gets overloaded, consider this: If we understood all there was to know about God, God wouldn't be God. We can't fully comprehend many things about God. But it's important to read the Book of Genesis for truth we *can* comprehend. Why? Because Genesis gives us clues into the mystery of life.

"In the beginning God *created*."

The fifth word of the Bible is God's first recorded action:

... "Let there be light"; ...

God *created*. Genesis 1 reveals how: God literally spoke the universe into being. With the words "And God said," the power of God's Word is demonstrated. God spoke, and things came to be: Light and darkness. Water, earth, and sky. Plants and trees. Stars and sunshine. Fish, birds, and animals. You and me. God said, "Let there be ...," and there was!

That same creative power is at work today. Every time a baby is born or a seed sprouts. When something that wasn't becomes something that is, it is a testimony to the creative power of God.

The first twenty-six verses describe how God created life. But the last seven verses show that God gave responsibility for that life to us. As the rulers of creation, we can plant trees and give birth to babies. We can cure diseases and create new species. We have the power to heal and create and give life, But with that comes the power to kill and destroy and bring death.

One look at the way we've handled this power makes us question whether human beings were worthy of such a task. God believed that we were. Perhaps that is the greatest miracle of all.

...And there was light.

1. Is the Creation story hard for you to believe? Why, or why not?

2. What evidence of God do you see in the world around you?

3. Would you say that human beings have done a good job or a bad job ruling the earth? How do you think God would answer that question?

Genesis 2

So the LORD God caused a deep sleep to fall upon the man, and he slept; then he took one of his ribs and closed up its place with flesh. And the rib that the LORD God had taken from the man he made into a woman and brought her to the man. Then the man said,

And God said...

> *"This at last is bone of my bones*
> *and flesh of my flesh;*
> *this one shall be called Woman,*
> *for out of Man this one was taken."*
> *Therefore a man leaves his father and his*
> *mother and clings to his wife, and they become*
> *one flesh. And the man and his wife were both*
> *naked, and were not ashamed.*

(Genesis 2:21-25, NRSV)

Volumes have been written about what *could have* happened in between the lines of Genesis. This book, however, will not be one of them. Instead, we will focus on what *did* happen in the lines of Genesis and see what lessons we can learn along the way.

Unlike the rest of creation, human beings were not spoken into existence. We were made by God's own hands. Genesis 1:26 alludes to this, but Genesis 2 describes it in detail. God forms the man first and places him in the Garden of Eden, surrounded by animals. Soon it becomes clear that even among the company of animals, Adam feels alone. (It's hard to relate to company that grunts, howls, screeches, and sniffs.) God realizes that this isn't good, so God forms the woman to come alongside of Adam. When

Adam sees her, he recognizes his perfect complement. He says, "This...is bone of my bones and flesh of my flesh." It may not be the most romantic poem, but it's Adam's way of high-fiving God and saying, "This is what I'm talking about!" (Let's hope that the woman felt the same way.)

...**"Let there be light";...**

By creating woman and man, God satisfied the human need for relationships. And God has been doing that ever since. We are given fathers and mothers, brothers and sisters, friends and partners, husbands and wives. These relationships bring joy and sorrow to our lives; but in them, we grow to become what we never could alone.

Genesis 2 also introduces us to one of life's greatest mysteries: the power of human choice. God introduces this power by planting a tree in the garden and telling Adam not to eat from it. By doing this, God gives Adam the freedom to choose right or wrong. This action sets the stage for the drama that occurs in Genesis 3.

We might wonder why God would allow the possibility of a wrong choice by putting that tree in the garden. But without that possibility, there would be no freedom—and that's the real message of Genesis 2. Human beings were created by God to be free. Obedience is our choice.

1. How does this Creation story differ from Genesis 1? How are they comparable?

...And there was light.

2. Why do you think the Bible has both Genesis 1 and 2? What does chapter 2 give us that chapter 1 doesn't include?

3. Why, do you think, did God give the possibility of choice by placing that tree in the garden? What would human beings be like if we couldn't choose wrong?

The Fall

Genesis 3

Now the serpent was more crafty than any of the wild animals the LORD God had made. He said to the woman, "Did God really say, 'You must not eat from any tree in the garden'?"

The woman said to the serpent, "We may eat fruit from the trees in the garden, but God did say, 'You must not eat fruit from the tree that is in the middle of the garden, and you must not touch it, or you will die.' "

And God said . . .

"You will not surely die," the serpent said to the woman. "For God knows that when you eat of it your eyes will be opened, and you will be like God, knowing good and evil."

When the woman saw that the fruit of the tree was good for food and pleasing to the eye, and also desirable for gaining wisdom, she took some and ate it. She also gave some to her husband, who was with her, and he ate it. (Genesis 3:1-6, NIV)

The drama of Genesis 3 unfolds with the introduction of the serpent. We can speculate as to how and why the serpent got there, but that would be guessing at what we don't know. What we do know is that the serpent came to counteract God's words and plant seeds of doubt in the woman and the man. And human beings have been dealing with this conflict ever since.

It would be easy to look at Adam and Eve and condemn them for making the choices they did—choices that ultimately altered the course of human life. Instead, I want to look at *how* it happened. I hope then that we can glean some truth to lean on when we find ourselves in a similar situation.

Notice the first words recorded from the serpent: "Did God really say . . . ?" Those same words echo in our brain when we are thinking about disobeying God. The serpent poses the question to make God look like the "Grand Depriver." "Did God really say that you're not supposed to eat from any tree in the garden?" How

. . ."Let there be light"; . . .

unreasonable God sounds! The question is a disguised lie, because God doesn't say that (see Genesis 2:16, 17).

Eve starts out well in her response, reaffirming the truth that God gave them permission to eat from every tree but one. If she had stayed right there—focusing on the freedom they had, rather than the restraint placed upon them—she might have responded differently. But the serpent is relentless. Temptation always is.

In verse 4, the serpent moves from questioning God's words to contradicting them altogether. The serpent makes it sound as though God's motive is to hold back goodness from Adam and Eve by restraining them. This is a strategy the enemy still uses, dangling immediate pleasures before us to make us question God's restraints. But remember this: Immediate pleasure often brings long-term pain, and sometimes we have to withstand immediate pain to secure long-term pleasure.

Adam and Eve ate from the tree, deciding that the taste of the sweet fruit was worth the risk. I wonder if they would still make that choice.

1. List the things that happened to Eve that made her give in to sin. What (if anything) could she have done differently?

...And there was light.

2. What caused Adam to eat from the tree? How should he have responded to Eve when she offered him the fruit?

3. What temptations in your life are difficult to resist? What can you learn from this chapter about how to stand strong against sin?

Cain and Abel

Genesis 4

Then the LORD said to Cain, "Why are you angry? Why is your face downcast? If you do what is right, will you not be accepted? But if you do not do what is right, sin is crouching at your door; it desires to have you, but you must master it.

Now Cain said to his brother Abel, "Let's go out to the field." And while they were in the field, Cain attacked his brother Abel and killed him.

And God said . . .

Then the LORD said to Cain, "Where is your brother Abel?"

"I don't know," he replied. "Am I my brother's keeper?"

(Genesis 4:6-9, NIV)

Genesis 4 tells the story of the first murder. It's impossible to count how many have taken place since. As I write this, the news is covering a murder trial involving a man accused of killing his wife and unborn child. The choices people make and the actions they take show the great risk God took in making human beings free. This story from Genesis illustrates that risk.

The chapter begins with joy, as Adam and Eve give birth to two boys, Cain and Abel. As they grow, Abel keeps the flocks while Cain works the soil. The time comes for each of them to offer a sacrifice to God, and the Lord looks with favor on Abel's sacrifice but not upon Cain's. We are given some clue as to why this happened when God says to Cain, "If you do what is right, will you not be accepted?" (verse 6). Somehow Cain's sacrifice is not right, and God gives him a chance to do it again.

But instead of focusing his attention on making a better sacrifice, Cain focuses his attention on his brother. In

. . . **"Let there be light";** . . .

doing so, he allows jealousy to get the best of him.

Has that ever happened to you? When a friend gets a better grade, a date with a person you like, or a position on a sports team you wanted, it's hard not to be jealous. Maybe you've thought that it would be nice if that friend just went away. Well Cain did more than think it; he made Abel go away—for good.

After Cain killed Abel, God comes to Cain with an interesting question: "Where is your brother?" God knows where Abel is, but God wants Cain to own up to his sin. Instead, Cain refuses to confess. He says, "I don't know. Am I my brother's keeper?" God doesn't answer, but it's clear that the answer is yes.

Cain is responsible for his actions because he *is* his brother's keeper. We all are. We may have the freedom to treat people the way we want, but there are consequences for treating them wrongly. And those consequences are felt by more than just us. Because of Cain's actions, Adam and Eve lost one of their sons. Abel lost his life. And even though Cain lived, he had to live with the guilt and separation that came from his choice.

And that might make you wonder whether Cain's loss wasn't the biggest of all.

1. Why do you think Abel's sacrifice was accepted but Cain's was not? What would have made Cain's sacrifice acceptable?

...And there was light.

2. How does the Lord's warning to Cain (verse 6) show God's love and care for him? How did Cain respond?

3. Have you ever been jealous of someone who did something better than you? What does this story teach you about how you should respond?

From Adam to Noah

Genesis 5

When Adam had lived 130 years, he had a son in his own likeness, in his own image; and he named him Seth. After Seth was born, Adam lived 800 years and had other sons and daughters. Altogether, Adam lived 930 years, and then he died....

When Enoch had lived 65 years, he became the father of Methuselah. And after he became the father of Methuselah, Enoch walked with God 300 years and had other sons and daughters. Altogether, Enoch lived 365 years. Enoch walked with God; then he was no more, because God took him away....

And God said ...

After Noah was 500 years old, he became the father of Shem, Ham and Japheth.

(Genesis 5:3-5, 21-24, 32, NIV)

One look at this chapter, and you probably have the impulse to skip it. I did. At first glance, genealogies are not exactly exciting. In fact, they're pretty boring. So why does the Bible have them?

Genealogies give us a sense of our history, and we can learn a lot by knowing where we came from. Have you ever explored your genealogy? My grandparents on my dad's side were Serbian; and because of that, I tan easily and have strong bones. My grandparents were Serbian Orthodox, so my parents had me baptized into the Christian faith as an infant. This set the tone for who I am today. Someday I'd like to go to Serbia to get a glimpse of my past—and more insight on how God made me to be.

Genealogies help you understand your past and give

you insights about your life. Genesis 5 is no different. By looking at the chain between Adam and Noah, we can observe some important facts. These facts help us understand where we all began.

... "Let there be light"; ...

First of all, you will notice that the chapter does not begin with Adam. The first genealogy begins with God. Ultimately it is God's image that we all bear—not Adam's or Eve's. And every one of us can trace our heritage back to that.

Notice that Cain is not mentioned as Adam's son; Seth is. This gives us some insight into the consequences of murder. Cain alienated himself from his family when he did what he did. And this chapter shows that he ended up disconnected from his heritage.

But the most important observation for us to notice is that only one person "walked with God" and that was Enoch (verses 22 and 24). This is an indication of the sorry state of humanity and a premonition for what's to come in Chapter 6. But what happens to Enoch in this chapter gives us all hope. Unlike every other person in the genealogy, Enoch did not die. God took him away.

This is the first hint we have that for those who walk with God, death is not the end of the story. And we all have a lot to learn from that.

1. Why do you think the Bible documents genealogies? Why are they important?

...And there was light.

2. What verses stand out to you in this genealogy? Why?

3. How much do you know of your genealogy? What, if anything, has it taught you about yourself?

The Consequence of Evil

Genesis 6

The LORD saw that the wickedness of humankind was great in the earth, and that every inclination of the thoughts of their hearts was only evil continually. And the LORD was sorry that he had made humankind on the earth, and it grieved him to his heart. So the LORD said, "I will blot out from the earth the human beings I have created—people together with animals and creeping things and birds of the air, for I am sorry that I have made them." But Noah found favor in the sight of the LORD.
(Genesis 6:5-8, NRSV)

And God said ...

This might be the saddest chapter in the Bible. In it, God faces the fallout of giving human beings freedom to choose and finding that they are choosing wrong. You can't help but know how grieved God must feel—especially since you know that God's heart wanted them to choose right.

It's probably a little like what it feels like to be a parent of a teenager. (Maybe this will help you understand yours.) You try to set the course for your children. You tell them what is right and wrong. You show them the consequences for bad behavior. But ultimately, they will grow up and do what they want—and you have to let go and watch them. This process can be painful for parents. But nothing could be more painful than what happened to God:

"The Lord saw that the wickedness of humankind was great in the earth, and that every inclination of the thoughts of their hearts was only evil continually." Read that sentence again. We need to meditate on this verse to fully understand what happens in this chapter. It's not as though God was unhappy because a few things had gone wrong. The whole thing had gone wrong. So God made the grave decision to begin again.

... "Let there be light"; ...

The grace in this chapter is seen in the fact that God would even want to begin again. God is unwilling to give up on humanity, even though humanity had obviously given up on God. However, one man stood apart as the exception; and he is the man God chooses to begin again.

Noah is introduced as a righteous, blameless man who—you guessed it—"walked with God." There's something about that phrase we need to understand. Throughout the Bible, this theme of walking with God carries great importance. Notice that it's not "standing with God" or "believing in God." It's a movement with God. Apparently, God wants to move with people throughout their lives. This is more than a one-time decision. It's an everyday decision we continually make.

For Noah, the decision to walk with God would lead him on an amazing journey. But the grief of this chapter is the tragic outcome for those who didn't make that choice.

1. Why do you think human beings became so evil? When did it start?

...And there was light.

2. Why didn't God destroy everyone and just start over with Creation? What did Noah do that made God want to spare him and his family?

3. On a scale of 1–10, do you think that God is more a God of judgment or a God of grace? (1 is judgment; 10 is grace.) How do you see evidence of both in this chapter?

The Flood

And Noah did all that the LORD had commanded him.
Noah was six hundred years old when the flood of waters came on the earth. And Noah with his sons and his wife and his sons' wives went into the ark to escape the waters of the flood. Of clean animals, and of animals that are not clean, and of birds, and of everything that creeps on the ground, two and two, male and

And God said... *female, went into the ark with Noah, as God had commanded Noah. And after seven days the waters of the flood came on the earth.* (Genesis 7:5-10, NRSV)

Let's just picture this scene for a minute. God has told Noah to build a 450-foot-long ark. But instead of having Noah build it next to water, God tells him that the water will come from the sky. If that weren't strange enough, Noah is told that before God brings the water, he has to get his family and two of every kind of creature on board the ark. Imagine how all of this must have looked to the people around him.

This is the first time in the Bible that we see someone called to act on faith. Noah is being asked by God not to trust what he sees, but to trust what he doesn't see—and to bank his life on this trust. Imagine for a moment if God hadn't come through. If Noah's family sat on that ark with all those animals and the rain never came, Noah would have been

the biggest fool on the planet. Instead, he and his family were the only ones left on the planet. And his trust in God paid off.

Sometimes God asks us to do things that seem to make no sense. If we obey and move forward in faith, we eventually  **..."Let there be light";...** see why. But we're called to act on faith *before* we see why. Every time we do this—and watch God come through—our faith gets a little bit stronger.

Exercising our faith is a little like exercising a muscle. The more we use our faith, the bigger our faith becomes. The opposite is also true. God wants our faith to increase so that we have the power to do great things. But the power comes from trusting God. This story shows that it is God's desire to use us in significant ways. God could have flooded the earth and started over without Noah's help. But God chose to partner with Noah and include him in the plan, instead. All Noah had to do was act on faith.

Acting on faith doesn't mean that things will be easy. It's difficult to imagine the horror that Noah and his family endured as they watched the flood cover the earth. While they reaped the benefits from living a life of faith, they saw the severe consequences of living a life without faith—and I'm sure that those images stayed with them forever. But those images also served as a reminder of God's deliverance.

As the flood arose, Noah and his family were the only ones left. And from that point on, Noah lived with the assurance that what God says God does.

1. What is the worst natural disaster you've ever witnessed? How did it make you feel?

...And there was light.

2. What do you think it was like for Noah and his family to watch the flood cover the earth?

3. What is the best adjective to describe how this chapter makes you feel about God? Why does it make you feel that way?

Promise and Prophesy

Genesis 8

But God remembered Noah and all the wild animals and all the domestic animals that were with him in the ark. And God made a wind blow over the earth, and the waters subsided; the fountains of the deep and the windows of the heavens were closed, the rain from the heavens was restrained, and the waters gradually receded from the earth. At the end of one hundred fifty days the waters had abated.
(Genesis 8:1-3, NRSV)

And God said…

After two chapters of sadness and destruction, Genesis 8 is a chapter of hope. It begins with three great words: "God remembered Noah." At first glance, it sounds odd, as though God had forgotten Noah and then suddenly remembered him. But that's not what the word *remember* means here.

Remember is an important word in the Old Testament. It means more than just recalling; it means being moved to action. Throughout the Bible, God's people are called to remember events that demonstrated God's kindness and character so that they will press on in their faith. But in this chapter, it is God who does the remembering. And after 150 days of silence, God is moved to act on Noah's behalf.

Noah's first great test of faith was belief that the water would come. But his second test of faith was belief that the water would recede. I can imagine that there were moments when his family thought that the flood would go on forever and eventually drown everyone on the ark. Maybe Noah felt that way too. But those were the moments when Noah could lean on his faith muscles and remember that God would come through.

… "Let there be light"; …

And God did come through, but it took a little while. (That's a good thing to remember about God.) First the water stopped. Then after some time passed, Noah sent a dove out through a window; and it brought back an olive leaf. A week later, Noah sent out the same dove and it didn't return. Then he knew that God's promise had been fulfilled.

The first lesson of this chapter is seeing how God remembers Noah, and acts on Noah's behalf. But the second lesson of the chapter is seeing how Noah remembers God, and acts on God's behalf. After the land dries and Noah and his family get off the ark, the first thing Noah does is build an altar to the Lord. And he makes a sacrifice for all God has done for them. In this act, Noah remembers God. And every time we worship God, we do the same.

Noah's act of worship pleases God so much, it moves God to make a promise never to destroy humanity again. It's a big promise, because God knows that humanity will continue to turn away. But there will be another plan in the future to take care of that— and it won't involve a flood. It will involve a cross. Because God will remember this promise.

1. What kind of bird did Noah use to find out that the water had receded? What do you think the significance was in that?

...And there was light.

2. What is the significance of "remembering" in this chapter? How does it lead to action for both Noah and God?

3. Have you ever remembered in a way that has moved you to action? If so, what did you do?

The Sign

Genesis 9

I will remember my covenant that is between me and you and every living creature of all flesh; and the waters shall never again become a flood to destroy all flesh. When the bow is in the clouds, I will see it and remember the everlasting covenant between God and every living creature of all flesh that is on the earth. God said to Noah, "This is the sign of the covenant that I have established between me and all flesh that is on the earth."
(Genesis 9:15-17, NRSV)

And God said . . .

What is a sign? It's a symbol that says something without words. When you see a gold band on the ring finger of someone's left hand, it's a sign of commitment. When you see four stars on a military uniform it's a sign of honor. When you see a medal worn around the neck of an athlete, it's a sign of accomplishment. All three of these signs—a ring, four stars, and a medal—do not carry the same meaning on their own. But when the ring is placed on a finger, the stars are placed on a uniform, and the medal is worn by an athlete, each conveys a message that speaks without words.

In this chapter, the rainbow is given as a sign that God will never again flood the earth. When the rainbow appears after the rain, God is fulfilling the promise that the rain will always stop. We don't have to worry that rain will continue indefinitely, because we are heirs to the promise given to Noah. And every time we see that rainbow in the sky, we remember God's words in this chapter.

. . . "Let there be light"; . . .

The promise God gives with the rainbow is referred to as a "covenant." Unlike a contract, which has to be kept by both parties to stay in place, a covenant is a promise that stands even if the other party fails to keep it. In this case, God makes a covenant with Noah that never again will all life be cut off by the waters of a flood.

It's interesting that before God makes this promise, Noah is

28

given some directions on how God would like for humans to behave—and some consequences if they choose not to behave this way. But the covenant stands separate from these conditions, and God promises to keep the covenant no matter what. It's an amazing statement of God's love.

Perhaps the most difficult part of this chapter is seeing how Noah behaves shortly after receiving this great promise. He plants a vineyard, drinks too much wine, and lies naked in front of his sons. Then, instead of owning his sin, he blames one of his sons for his embarrassment. So, in the story of Noah, we see an example of what God already knew—that humans, no matter how good, will also act evil. And yet God's promise prevails.

The next time you see a rainbow, remember that.

...And there was light.

1. How is a covenant different from a contract? How would things be different if God had made a contract with Noah, instead?

2. Why, do you think, did Noah act the way he did at the end of this chapter? What warning does that give us about ourselves?

3. The next time you see a rainbow, what will you remember about this chapter?

Territories and Nations

Genesis 10

These are the descendants of Noah's sons, Shem, Ham, and Japheth; children were born to them after the flood.
These are the families of Noah's sons, according to their genealogies, in their nations; and from these the nations spread abroad on the earth after the flood.
(Genesis 10:1, 32, NRSV)

And God said...

Twice in the previous chapter God said to Noah, "Be fruitful and multiply." This chapter shows that Noah did just that. The many births show that God brought new life after the destruction of the flood. This is also the way God works in our individual lives. When something dies, something else begins. And as long as we're here, we always have hope that God will bring us new life.

The genealogy presented in chapter 5 followed one line from Adam to Noah. This chapter begins with Noah, but the genealogy is divided into three sections, following each of Noah's sons. Each section reveals the beginning of a different group of people—and these groups will eventually spread out to populate the earth. For the first time, we are introduced to the terms *territory* and *clans*. This indicates the beginning of separation and distinction amongst people, which will become more prominent as the earth becomes more populated.

Probably the most significant aspect of this genealogy is the  ..."Let there be light"; ... introduction of the Shemites, who will later be known as Semites, or Jews. Although all three lineages of Noah's sons are mentioned in this chapter, only Shem's line will be followed. The stories of Genesis will be the stories of the descendants of Shem. The Bible gives us God's wisdom and truth through the stories of the Jews, and much of Genesis is filled with these stories.

One day Shem's line will produce a man who will embody God's wisdom and truth. He will be born into a Jewish family, but his origins will be from God. His birth will be the beginning of a covenant that will be extended to all people. But you'll have to read ahead to the New Testament for that story.

In this book, we're exploring the stories of Genesis. And we'll discover the richness these stories can bring to our relationship with God. The word *genesis* comes from the Greek word *geneseos,* which means "birth," "genealogy," or "history of origin." All three meanings are present in this chapter. Because this chapter shows us where we began.

1. After such a huge tragedy, how does this chapter give us a sense of hope? What does that tell you about God?

...And there was light.

2. What are the similarities between Adam and Noah? What are the differences?

3. What is the most important fact that stands out to you in this chapter? Why?

The Tower of Babel

Genesis 11

Now the whole earth had one language and the same words....And they said to one another, "Come, let us make bricks, and burn them thoroughly." And they had brick for stone, and bitumen for mortar. Then they said, "Come, let us build ourselves a city, and a tower with its top in the heavens, and let us make a name for ourselves; otherwise we shall be scattered abroad upon the face of the whole earth."

And God said ...

The LORD came down to see the city and the tower, which mortals had built. And the LORD said, "Look, they are one people, and they have all one language; and this is only the beginning of what they will do; nothing that they propose to do will now be impossible for them."
(Genesis 11:1, 3-6, NRSV)

Have you ever tried to talk to someone who doesn't speak your language? It can be frustrating and comical. The first thing I do is talk louder as though the person might understand if I speak up. Then I resort to using my hands to act out the words. The problem is, when people try to guess what I'm saying, it doesn't really help because I don't understand them!

Language is a powerful tool. It can bond people together, or cause people to live apart. Countries are separated, and people within countries form separate communities—all because of language. However, this chapter speaks of a time when everyone in the world spoke the same language.

Genesis 11 begins with the sentence "Now the whole world had one language and the same words." Imagine what they could accomplish! People came together to create and build, which was not a bad thing. What was bad was their motivation for doing it. Instead of doing it to glorify God, they did it to glorify themselves. So God decided to put humans in their place.

... "Let there be light"; ...

Human power looks pretty good until God's power comes in and dominates it. In this chapter, it must have been kind of humorous. The people are all together building this huge tower, when suddenly they can't communicate. Someone asks for a brick and is handed a ladder. Then that person turns to ask someone else, and a third person gives them some tar. Imagine the frustration and chaos. In an instant, their power is abruptly limited. A greater power has taken control.

Because human beings can build and create, we have this sense that we control the world. But no matter how powerful our buildings are, they can be destroyed. No matter how great our technology is, it will soon be replaced. No matter how wonderful our inventions are, they will eventually be outdone. The longer we live, the more we realize that our power is limited. And this chapter of Genesis gives us good reason why.

Human power on it's own can be destructive. History has given us evidence of that. But history has also shown us that human power, whether for good or evil, is limited. God's power always has the last word.

And sometimes God has to take away our words to prove it.

1. How would the world be different if we all spoke the same language? Do you think that it would be better or worse?

...And there was light.

2. Have you ever been someplace where you couldn't speak the language? If so, how did it make you feel?

3. Do you think that knowing another language gives you more power? Why, or why not?

The Call of Abram

Genesis 12

Now the LORD said to Abram, "Go from your country and your kindred and your father's house to the land that I will show you. I will make of you a great nation, and I will bless you, and make your name great, so that you will be a blessing. I will bless those who bless you, and the one who curses you I will curse; and in you all the families of the earth shall be blessed."

And God said…

So Abram went, as the LORD had told him; and Lot went with him. Abram was seventy-five years old when he departed from Haran. (Genesis 12:1-4, NRSV)

Imagine if God called you to leave everything that was familiar in your life and go somewhere you've never been. That's what happens in this chapter. The first we hear of Abram, he is given a command to leave his country, his people, and his household. And the amazing thing was, *he went!*

We don't know anything about Abram, but we can assume from his response that he was a man of faith. The next several chapters will show us how his faith evolves.

God begins by taking Abram on a journey that requires his trust. And in a sense, that's how God begins with all of us.

When we are called to follow God, we are called to leave our old lives behind. In Abram's case, this meant physically leaving. For us, it may or may not be the same. Instead of a move out of the country, it could be a move out of a relationship. Instead of a move away, it could be a move that sets you apart. It may not be a physical move, but a spiritual move. And sometimes that's the biggest move of all.

…"Let there be light";…

Because it doesn't just change your geography; it changes you.

What we learn in this chapter is that God's journey with us begins with our response. Abram could have said no, and the chapter would have ended right there. Instead, Abram obeyed and left. And the coming chapters will show that God has a great adventure in store for him.

Adventures always begin with risk. For Abram that meant leaving behind a life he knows for a life about which he knows nothing. However, he knows enough about God to take that risk. Do you?

It's comforting to see in this chapter that even though Abram is a man of faith, he struggles too. That's good news for you and me. As you read on, you will see that Abram doesn't always respond with faith. There are times when he responds with fear; but when that happens, God stays with Abram. And Abram stays with God. That's what it means to live the journey.

It's the journey that teaches us a life of faith. Our job is to simply stay on it.

1. Have you ever moved somewhere new? If so, what was the hardest part about the move?

...And there was light.

2. Why, do you think, was Abram able to do what God was asking him to do? What does that tell you about his relationship with God?

3. On a scale of 1–10, how far are you willing to go with God? (1=nowhere; 10=anywhere) What would it take for you to go farther?

Letting Go and Letting God

Genesis 13

Now Lot, who went with Abram, also had flocks and herds and tents, so that the land could not support both of them living together; for their possessions were so great that they could not live together, and there was strife between the herders of Abram's livestock and the herders of Lot's livestock. At that time the Canaanites and the Perizzites lived in the land.

And God said ...

Then Abram said to Lot, "Let there be no strife between you and me, and between your herders and my herders; for we are kindred. Is not the whole land before you? Separate yourself from me. If you take the left hand, then I will go to the right; or if you take the right hand, then I will go to the left."
(Genesis 13:5-9, NRSV)

This chapter teaches us a very important lesson, a lesson we continue to learn throughout our lives. Abram will too. And his first opportunity to learn it is in this chapter.

Abram and his nephew Lot have acquired so much that it has become too hard to travel together. It is time to part ways. Because Abram is the patriarch and the elder of the two, it is his right to decide how this will happen. But Abram isn't a person who lives by his rights.

We saw this in Abram's decision to follow God. He let go of his rights to his land and let God decide where he should go. Here Abram makes a similar choice. Instead of choosing the land himself, he lets Lot make the decision. When Abram lets go of his control, he puts the situation in God's control. And the outcome shows that he made the right choice.

After Lot chooses the best land and goes his way, the Lord informs Abram that all the land will eventually be his. But Abram doesn't get that promise

... "Let there be light"; ...

until he gives the best land away. If Abram had known that this was going to happen, his generosity to Lot would have been a lot easier. Instead, it was a sacrifice.

The sacrifice is what God honors. God wants us to give up everything we hold on to so that we can learn how to hold things loosely. The minute our grip around something gets too tight, we lose our proper perspective. Love turns to possessiveness, wealth turns to greed, and gifts turn to expectations. When this happens, we are the ones who lose out. The amazing thing is that once we are willing to let go, we gain more than we had before. But this can only happen if we truly let go.

The more you love something, the harder it is to give it up. Abram will learn that lesson down the road. For now, all he has to let go of is a piece of land. But letting go of that land starts a process in Abram, and it will eventually lead him to be able to let go of a piece of his heart.

Until then, God will work on Abram, shaping and molding his faith until he becomes all that God wants him to be. That's the way God works in all of us. Our part is to let go, trust God, and watch.

1. Why do you think Abram gave Lot his choice of land? How do you think being given the choice made Lot feel?

...And there was light.

2. Why is it important for us to learn to let go? Why does God want us to hold things loosely?

3. Of what in your life is hardest for you to let go? What steps could you take to loosen your grip?

Courage and Commitment

Genesis 14

When Abram heard that his nephew had been taken captive, he led forth his trained men, born in his house, three hundred eighteen of them, and went in pursuit as far as Dan. He divided his forces against them by night, he and his servants, and routed them and pursued them to Hobah, north of Damascus. Then he brought back all the goods, and also brought back his nephew Lot with his goods, and the women and the people.
(Genesis 14:14-16, NRSV)

And God said...

Up until now, our picture of Abram has been as a wandering shepherd. But everything changes in this chapter. Here we discover that Abram can also be a mighty warrior; and he is willing to put his life on the line for the people he loves.

It's hard to understand exactly what is going on in this chapter, but there has been some sort of rebellion and nine kings are battling for power. One of the kings is from Sodom, which affects Abram's nephew Lot, since he has made his home there. The king from Sodom is on the losing side, and Lot is carried off as part of the prize. That's when Abram shows up.

In this chapter we learn that Abram is not just a man of faith, he is a man of courage. When Abram hears that Lot has been taken hostage, he immediately goes to battle on Lot's behalf. This shows the extent of his loyalty. Not only is Abram loyal to God, he is loyal to the people who need him. And he is willing to make sacrifices for their protection.

As I write this, our country is involved in a war that has required  ... **"Let there be light"**; ... many people to make such sacrifices. Thousands of soldiers have left the comfort of their homes to fight for people who need them. Their courage and commitment have been displayed in their sacrifice. It's in such sacrifices that our true nature is revealed.

Abram made a great sacrifice by fighting for Lot. He could have rationalized that Lot blew it by choosing the wrong land.

Instead, Abram took responsibility for Lot's misfortune; and he put his own well-being on the line to get him back.

Abram's commitment to Lot was a reflection of his commitment to God. And Abram was willing to step out of his comfort zone to fulfill it. Abram is quite a soldier, and he executes the attack very successfully. The goods are recovered, Lot is returned, and the king of Sodom is so pleased that he wants to reward Abram.

But Abram doesn't accept anything for his own honor. Instead, he gives a sacrifice to honor God. Abram knows where the reward belongs. And the next chapter will prove him right.

1. Why, do you think, did Abram put his life on the line to rescue Lot? What does that say about his character?

...And there was light.

2. Do you think that loyalty requires courage? Why?

3. Has there ever been a time when you've put yourself on the line because of your loyalty to someone? For whom in your life would you be willing to do that?

Unfulfilled Promises

Genesis 15

But Abram said, "O Lord GOD, what will you give me, for I continue childless, and the heir of my house is Eliezer of Damascus?" And Abram said, "You have given me no offspring, and so a slave born in my house is to be my heir." But the word of the LORD came to him, "This man shall not be your heir; no one but your very own issue shall be your heir." He brought him **And God said ...** *outside and said, "Look toward heaven and count the stars, if you are able to count them." Then he said to him, "So shall your descendants be." And he believed the LORD; and the LORD reckoned it to him as righteousness.*

(Genesis 15:2-6, NRSV)

After Abram gives his reward to God in the previous chapter, God comes to reward Abram. The problem is that the reward takes the shape of an unfulfilled promise. When God says to Abram, "I am your shield; your reward shall be very great" (verse 1), Abram questions that promise. He has been told repeatedly that he will be blessed with offspring, and still he remains childless. So it's understandable that Abram would question God. The great thing is that God lets him!

Many times God makes promises that require us to have faith. The more challenging our circumstances become, the harder it is to have faith. As time passes, it gets more and more difficult to believe; but God grows our faith during these times. If we continue to trust God and these promises are eventually fulfilled, we have a confidence in God that can happen no other way.

That's what God wanted for Abram. And that's what God wants for you and me. As I write this, I am living with the unfulfilled promise of marriage.  ... "Let there be light"; ... I have dated, I have been engaged, and still I remain unmarried.

Two years ago, I was speaking at a seminar and a woman approached me with some words God had laid on her heart. She told me that God was going to bring me a husband. Through all my confusing circumstances, I have carried those words as an encouragement not to give up.

But there have been many times I have wanted to cry out to God with my questions.

The great news about this chapter is that we can cry out with our questions. And God encourages us to hold on to hope. For Abram, God did this through the stars in the sky. (verse 5) God did something similar for me. One night while I was staring at the stars, God used the constellation of Orion to speak to my heart. To this day, when I see that man formed by the stars, it encourages me that God is at work bringing the right man into my life. God has given me that symbol as a promise of hope.

That may be hard to believe, but *you* don't have to believe because that promise is for *me*. God simply wants you to open your own eyes and heart to receive *your* promises. And even if your promises take a while to come to pass, the encouragement of this chapter is to never give up.

Abram "*believed* the LORD." (verse 6) Will you?

1. Why was Abram considered righteous?

...And there was light.

2. Is there a connection between faith and righteousness? If so, what is it?

3. What promises has God given you? Do you believe that God will fulfill those promises in your life?

Hagar and Ishmael

Genesis 16

Now Sarai, Abram's wife, bore him no children. She had an Egyptian slave-girl whose name was Hagar, and Sarai said to Abram, "You see that the LORD has prevented me from bearing children; go in to my slave-girl; it may be that I shall obtain children by her." And Abram listened to the voice of Sarai. So, after Abram had lived ten years in the land of Canaan, Sarai, Abram's wife, took Hagar the Egyptian, her slave-girl, and gave her to her husband Abram as a wife. He went in to Hagar, and she conceived; and when she saw that she had conceived, she looked with contempt on her mistress.
(Genesis 16:1-4, NRSV)

And God said ...

Sometimes we have the patience to wait for God's plan. This chapter shows what can happen when we don't.

It's completely understandable that Abram and Sarai would get to this place. It's been many years since God promised them an heir, and they are starting to question God's promise. So Sarai comes up with a plan to help God along.

Notice the process that Sarai goes through to make this decision. She starts by saying, "The LORD has prevented me from bearing children" (verse 2). Instead of seeing her circumstances as something that God will work through, she sees her circumstances as something God has sentenced her to; and this perspective makes all the difference. Once our circumstances cause us to question God's goodness, we are in danger of diminishing our faith. And nothing has the potential to do this more than a long wait.

Sarai felt (with good reason) that she had waited long enough. So instead of staying on God's timeline, she attempts to  **... "Let there be light"; ...** bring God's promise on her timeline. The plan is logical enough: Abram and Sarai will have a surrogate child (through Hagar) to fulfill God's promise. But Sarai doesn't think through the emotional impact of her plan. Eventually, Hagar resents Sarai, Sarai blames Abram, and Abram lets Sarai mistreat Hagar. What started out to be a solution has created more problems. This is what happens when we take over God's plan.

The good news is that even when we preempt God's plan, God works it into a bigger plan—and the original plan is not lost. Even though Hagar's child is not the child of promise, a new promise is extended to her child. And God's grace covers both Hagar and her child.

Sarai could never have known the problems Hagar's pregnancy would create. The birth of Ishmael and his descendants would spark a conflict between two nations (Arabs and Israelis) that continues to this very day. It all began in this chapter—with one woman taking God's job into her own hands.

But in the end, God showed Sarai who was in charge. And she would eventually see through her 90-year-old body just how powerful God could be.

1. What motivated Sarai to do what she did? Can you relate to her at all?

...And there was light.

2. On a scale of 1–10, how patient are you in waiting on God? (1=very impatient; 10=very patient) How does your patience compare to Sarai's?

3. In what area of your life do you struggle with waiting on God? How does this chapter help you in your struggle?

Names of Promise

"As for me, this is my covenant with you: You shall be the ancestor of a multitude of nations. No longer shall your name be Abram, but your name shall be Abraham; for I have made you the ancestor of a multitude of nations. I will make you exceedingly fruitful; and I will make nations of you, and kings shall come from you...."

And God said...

God said to Abraham, "As for Sarah your wife, you shall not call her Sarai, but Sarah shall be her name. I will bless her, and moreover I will give you a son by her. I will bless her, and she shall give rise to nations; kings of peoples shall come from her." (Genesis 17:4-6, 15-16, NRSV)

Have you ever asked your parents how you got your name? There might be more to it than you think. I got my name from a character in a movie. For my dad, this name represented the ideal woman. And it was a symbol of what my parents wanted me to become.

In this chapter, Abram and Sarai are given new names. The new names are symbols of what God wants them to become. Abram is given the name Abraham, meaning "father of many." The only problem is, Abraham is 99 years old and the father of one. And that one is not his true heir. Sarai's name is now Sarah, and she is going to be the mother of nations. The problem is, Sarah is 89 years old. If biology has anything to do with it, she's not going to be anyone's mother. That hope has long since died.

It's no wonder that Abraham falls face down when he hears this announcement from God. I would too. After all this time, God is still giving this promise. So Abraham decides to reason with God: How about Ishmael? Wouldn't it be easier to make him the promised son? Couldn't he live under God's blessing?

... "Let there be light"; ...

I love God's response to Abraham: "Yes...but" (verse 19). Ishmael will live under God's blessing, but that doesn't change what God is still going to do. Now that the circumstances are impossible, God is in prime position to show up. And God loves to do that. You'll discover that as you walk in faith.

Abraham and Sarah may have given up on God, but God hasn't given up on them. There is a story unfolding beyond anything they could have asked or imagined. That's what makes it so great. Abraham and Sarah are barren, childless, and elderly; yet they are still to become the father and mother of all nations. The question is: How?

God doesn't answer that question. But the question God does answer is: When? Finally, the promise comes with a time frame. (I'll bet Abraham appreciated that.) Abraham is told that this time next year, he and Sarah will become parents for the very first time (verse 21).

Time to clear the cobwebs off the nursery. Abraham and Sarah are about to live up to their names.

1. Why did God change Sarah and Abraham's names? How, do you think, did it affect them?

...And there was light.

2. Why couldn't Ishmael be the promised son? How would that have altered God's plan?

3. If God were to give you a new name based on a hope for your life, what would it be?

Is Anything too Hard?

Genesis 18

Then the LORD said, "I will surely return to you about this time next year, and Sarah your wife will have a son."

Now Sarah was listening at the entrance to the tent, which was behind him. Abraham and Sarah were already old and well advanced in years, and Sarah was past the age of childbearing.

And God said . . .

So Sarah laughed to herself as she thought, "After I am worn out and my master is old, will I now have this pleasure?"

Then the LORD said to Abraham, "Why did Sarah laugh and say, 'Will I really have a child, now that I am old?' Is anything too hard for the LORD? I will return to you at the appointed time next year and Sarah will have a son."

(Genesis 18:10-14, NIV)

Up until now, we've seen Abraham and Sarah's promise through the eyes of Abraham. But in this chapter, we get to see it through the eyes of Sarah. Three mysterious visitors have come; and while Sarah is busy cooking, she overhears the men talking about her. So she does what anyone would do in this situation—she moves closer so she can listen in.

The men tell Abraham that this time next year Sarah will have a son. In the past, this news would have brought hope. Now all Sarah can do is laugh. She looks at her 90-year-old body and starts to chuckle. Then she looks at Abraham's 100-year-old body, and her laughter grows. The visitor hears her and asks Abraham, "Why did Sarah laugh?" If I were Abraham, I would have replied, "Wouldn't you?"

It's at that point in the story that Abraham and Sarah are met with one of my favorite verses: "Is anything too hard for the LORD?" Their story will answer that question. But in the meantime, they're free to laugh.

That's what's

. . . "Let there be light"; . . .

great about this story. Sarah is embarrassed by her laughter and tries to cover it up. But the Lord wants Sarah to admit her laughter. After all, it is pretty funny. Can you picture your great-grandmother pregnant? How could you not laugh?

I think that God delights in doing the impossible. And the impossible makes us laugh. After all the crying Sarah has done, a hearty laugh must have felt so good. And God wanted her to admit it. You can hear it in their exchange. She says "I did not laugh." And the Lord says, "Yes you did laugh!"(verse 15). It's not really reprimanding, it's teasing. And I think that the Lord simply wanted Sarah to acknowledge the laughter.

After all the time Abraham and Sarah spent despairing for a child, God wants them to revel in their joy. It's the same for you and me. The celebration is part of the trial; and when the sorrow has been great, the joy should be even greater.

The Lord wanted Abraham and Sarah to start feeling their joy now. The baby was still to come, but the joy of anticipation was here.

1. Why, do you think, did Sarah laugh when she heard the news? Would you have laughed if you were her?

...And there was light.

2. Do you think that God was angry with Sarah for laughing? Why, or why not?

3. What in your life do you feel is "too hard" for God? How does this chapter help your faith?

Leaving Evil Behind

When morning dawned, the angels urged Lot, saying, "Get up, take your wife and your two daughters who are here, or else you will be consumed in the punishment of the city." But he lingered; so the men seized him and his wife and his two daughters by the hand, the LORD being merciful to him, and they brought him out and left him outside the city. When they had brought them outside,

And God said . . .

they said, "Flee for your life; do not look back or stop anywhere in the Plain; flee to the hills, or else you will be consumed."
(Genesis 19:15-17, NRSV)

This story takes us back to Lot, who has settled in the land of Sodom. The Lord has told Abraham that Sodom and Gomorrah are going to be destroyed for their sin. Abraham has asked that any righteous people be spared. God honors Abraham's request—and that's where this chapter begins.

It's almost like a scene from a trashy movie. Two angels arrive to rescue Lot and his family. While the angels are inside Lot's house, the men of Sodom demand to have sex with them. It's a shocking scene, but it gives us a picture of how sinful Sodom had become. Lot's initial answer reveals an awareness of right and wrong. He says, "Do not act so wickedly." But in his sickness, he offers his daughters instead (verse 8). In the end, the men are not interested in

Lot's daughters; they want the men inside. That's when all hell breaks loose—literally.

The angels reveal their strength as they pull Lot away from the men and strike the men with blindness. (Kind of alters your picture of floating

. . . "Let there be light"; . . .

people with harps and wings, doesn't it?)

In an instant, Lot is told to pack up his family and run. But he cannot convince his sons-in-law to go with him. The fact that no one takes Lot seriously is a sign of how weak his character had become.

Since Lot is unable to gather his family, the angels do it for him. They grab Lot, his wife, and his daughters and instruct them to flee and not look back. Lot's wife cannot do it. She turns her head, and her hesitation destroys her. The more we long for our sins, the harder it is to leave them. In Lot's wife's case, it left her dead.

The chapter ends much like it begins—with desperation and disgust. Lot's daughters believe that their only chance to bear children is with their own father. So in a drunken stupor, Lot complies. It's a fitting end to a pathetic life and reveals what happens when we make our home in sin. Hopefully, it's a lesson not to.

1. Do you think that God was cruel for destroying Sodom? Why, or why not?

...And there was light.

2. How was Lot affected by living in Sodom? Do you think that his surroundings changed him and his family?

3. Is there a place in your life like Sodom? How does this chapter encourage you to stay away?

Fear and Faith

Genesis 20

Abraham said of his wife Sarah, "She is my sister." And King Abimelech of Gerar sent and took Sarah. But God came to Abimelech in a dream by night, and said to him, "You are about to die because of the woman whom you have taken; for she is a married woman...."

And God said ...

Then Abimelech called Abraham, and said to him, "What have you done to us? How have I sinned against you, that you have brought such great guilt on me and my kingdom? You have done things to me that ought not to be done."
(Genesis 20:2-3, 9, NRSV)

Apparently, Sarah still has it. At least, that's what Abraham thinks. (I hope that my husband will feel the same way.) Abraham is still telling people that Sarah is his sister, because he's afraid that someone might kill him to get her. (This happened once before in Genesis 12:10-20.) The problem is that the king ends up taking Sarah, not knowing that she's a married woman. You'd think that since she is 90 years old, men would be less interested in her. But this chapter shows that they still are.

King Abimelech sends for Sarah, and Abraham lets her go. Abraham is afraid to tell the truth. These people do not fear God, so he doesn't feel that God will be able to protect him.

Therefore, Abraham decides to protect himself. Ultimately his theory is proved wrong, because God breaks through and protects him anyway. Abraham is put to shame—all because he didn't rely on his faith.

... "Let there be light"; ...

We can understand Abraham's dilemma. Sometimes we look at our circumstances and think that we need to take control. But faith is letting God take control. No matter how fearful we are, we have to trust that God will come through. When we don't, we not only miss out on seeing God's faithfulness, we miss out on being a witness. That's what happened to Abraham.

Abimelech never got to see Abraham's faith. Instead, he was a victim of Abraham's lack of faith. Abraham had gone through the same circumstances with Pharaoh in Genesis 12, but Abraham still didn't get it. For that reason, God will continue to work on Abraham's faith.

The journey of faith is facing our fears and letting God work through them. When we manage our fears ourselves, we never really get over them. And that's not how God wants us to live. If you are really afraid to do something, there's a chance that that's exactly what God wants you to do. When you do it and God takes you through it, you will know God in a deeper way. And that's the ultimate goal of our lives.

Abraham might not have passed the test of faith this time. But with God, there will be another chance. There always is.

1. Would you describe Abraham as faithful or fearful? Why?

...And there was light.

2. Why do you think it's hard for Abraham to trust God in this chapter? What is he afraid will happen?

3. What is the hardest thing for you to trust God with? How can you make a step toward trusting God more this week?

The Laughter of God's Joy

Genesis 21

The LORD dealt with Sarah as he had said, and the LORD did for Sarah as he had promised. Sarah conceived and bore Abraham a son in his old age, at the time of which God had spoken to him. Abraham gave the name Isaac to his son whom Sarah bore him....

Now Sarah said, "God has brought laughter for me; everyone who hears will laugh with me."

(Genesis 21:1-3, 6, NIV)

And God said...

The time has finally come. A twenty-five-year promise is finally fulfilled. How long Sarah and Abraham have agonized. How many times they had given up. But now the impossible has happened, and a son is born into their home!

They named the boy Isaac, which means "laughter." It signifies the joy and humor of his birth. Sarah acknowledges this by saying, "God has brought me laughter, and everyone who hears about this will laugh with me." She is no longer sensitive about the delay of God's timing. She is overjoyed at what that timing produced. The timing of Isaac's arrival shows that God revels in doing the impossible. Circumstances don't stop God's promises. God's promises are powerful enough to break through.

The joy of Isaac's birth was magnified by the sorrow that preceded it. If Isaac had been born at the usual time in the usual way, his birth wouldn't have produced as much joy as it did. The fact that Abraham and Sarah went through so much  ... "Let there be light"; ... pain only increased their happiness when the trial was over. When Isaac was born, all they could do was laugh. And Isaac's name is a testimony to that fact.

The sad note in this story is what happens when we rush God's promise, only to regret it when God's promise comes through. Hagar and Ishmael are a reminder of Sarah's impatience and of how our choices can complicate God's plan. Now that Sarah has her own son, she has no room for the son she helped to create. She wants to banish Hagar and Ishmael. Abraham is distressed by this, because Ishmael is his son. The joy God brought to Sarah is complicated by circumstances Sarah brought upon herself. It's a lesson to trust God's timing—no matter how long that timing might take.

The good news is that even when we complicate our lives with our actions, God covers those actions with grace. God doesn't allow Hagar and Ishmael to be victims of Sarah's mistake, and Abraham is promised that both sons will become great nations. God is able to weave in the mistake, without losing sight of the plan. Nevertheless, the mistake did have consequences that would be felt for years to come.

But for now, Abraham's home was filled with laughter. And after twenty-five years of tears, that laughter must have felt good.

1. Do you think that Abraham and Sarah were more joyful than most parents? Why?

...And there was light.

2. What is the most amazing thing you've seen God do? How does it compare with what God did in this chapter?

3. If you could ask God for a miracle, what would it be? Do you believe that God has the power to do it? How does this chapter encourage your faith?

Abraham's Test

Some time later God tested Abraham. He said to him, "Abraham!"
"Here I am," he replied.
Then God said, "Take your son, your only son, Isaac, whom you
love, and go to the region of Moriah. Sacrifice him there as a burnt
offering on one of the mountains I will tell you about."

And God said . . .

Early the next morning Abraham got up and saddled his donkey. He took with him two of his servants and his son Isaac. When he had cut enough wood for the burnt offering, he set out for the place God had told him about.
(Genesis 22:1-3, NIV)

Nothing was more precious to Abraham than his son Isaac. He was more than a son; he was the fulfillment of a lifelong promise. For years, Abraham had prayed and waited, agonized and waited, cried out and waited. And finally, Isaac had come. The joy Abraham felt! The laughter he and Sarah shared. The miracle they had witnessed. Until. . . .

God tells Abraham to take that son—his beloved son—up a mountain, and sacrifice him. Imagine the emotions that must have welled up inside of Abraham. How could God be asking this? It seems like some kind of sick joke. After all their waiting . . . now this? We don't know Abraham's thoughts, but we do know his actions. "Early the next morning Abraham got up and saddled his donkey"

(verse 3). No matter how he felt, Abraham obeyed—that shows you the measure of his faith.

Here we see God's most difficult and important lesson, a lesson I'm learning right now. A year and a half ago, I was engaged.

. . . "Let there be light"; . . .

After waiting so many years, it was the fulfillment of my dreams. But my fiancé was called to Iraq; and while he was there, we grew more and more distant. Finally, it became clear that I needed to take off my ring. God was telling me to let go and trust that, whatever happened, God was going to take care of it. It wasn't mine to take care of anymore.

It was hard. After waiting so long to be married, I couldn't understand why I had to give it up. But I knew that if I held on, I might miss out on God's plan. Whether it's a different relationship—or some other circumstance—I don't have the answer yet. But part of God's plan is the willingness to trust when we don't have the answers. That's when our faith really counts.

Certainly, Abraham showed tremendous faith when he made his way up that mountain. When Isaac asked him where the lamb was that they were sacrificing, Abraham said, "God . . . will provide" (verse 8). Abraham knew that God would take care of it, even if he wasn't sure how.

That is the definition of *faith*. God wants us to experience what faith can produce. The more we trust God, the more God can do in our lives. Abraham knew that. I want to know that too.

1. How do you think Abraham felt about God when God asked him to sacrifice Isaac? How would you have felt?

...And there was light.

2. Why, do you think, did Abraham obey so quickly? What does that tell you about Abraham's faith?

3. What would be hardest for you to sacrifice? Would you be willing to sacrifice it if God were to ask you to?

Saying Goodbye

Genesis 23

Sarah lived one hundred twenty-seven years; this was the length of Sarah's life. And Sarah died at Kiriath-arba (that is, Hebron) in the land of Canaan; and Abraham went in to mourn for Sarah and to weep for her. Abraham rose up from beside his dead, and said to the Hittites, "I am a stranger and an alien residing among you;

And God said...

give me property among you for a burying place, so that I may bury my dead out of my sight." (Genesis 23:1-4, NRSV)

Last summer, my friend Vivian lost her husband. They had been married for thirty-nine years. She felt great pain over his death. That's because of the joy she experienced while he was here.

The more you love, the harder it is to let go. It's a lesson we learn throughout our lives. Abraham had to learn this lesson too. Over and over again, God asked him to let go ... of his land, of his plans, of his son Ishmael, of his son Isaac. Now, Abraham must let go of Sarah too.

God gave these things to Abraham to enjoy, learn from, and love; but these things are not his. They are God's. Just as Abraham opened his hands to accept them, he needs to open his hands to give them back. We all do. At some point, we must say goodbye; and

sometimes it happens sooner than we would like.

For my friend Vivian, it happened last summer. Quite suddenly, her husband was gone. He was killed in a plane crash, doing what he loved. But she was left with a tremen-

..."Let there be light";...

dous loss. Because of her faith, she can grieve with grace and hope. Because of her love, she has shed many tears. She loved the gift God gave her, and her tears are the expression of her gratitude. Abraham's tears are the same.

We know by now that Abraham trusts God. That's why this chapter is so tender. When Sarah dies, Abraham weeps. It's the only time that we see Abraham's emotion. He accepts Sarah's death as part of God's plan, but his tears reveal how sad he is to let her go. After he weeps, Abraham lays Sarah's body in his family's burial ground. And says goodbye to his partner and friend.

Now Abraham has to learn to live alone. Ultimately, we all do. We are given mothers and fathers, sisters and brothers, husbands and wives, friends and partners. But these people are not ours to keep; they're ours to learn from and enjoy. We should never take them for granted, because someday they'll be gone. It's usually at that moment that we realize how much we loved them while they were here.

Just ask my friend Vivian.

...And there was light.

1. Have you ever lost someone close to you? If so, what emotions did you feel?

2. How have you seen evidence of Abraham and Sarah's love throughout Genesis? Do you know any couples like them?

3. Who would be the hardest person for you to lose? How does this chapter help you appreciate your relationships?

A Perfect Match

Abraham said to his servant, the oldest of his house, who had charge of all that he had, "Put your hand under my thigh and I will make you swear by the LORD, the God of heaven and earth, that you will not get a wife for my son from the daughters of the Canaanites, among whom I live, but will go to my country and to my kindred and get a wife for my son Isaac." (Genesis 24:2-4, NRSV)

And God said...

Have you ever seen *Fiddler on the Roof*? There's a song in it that reminds me of this passage. I can see Abraham grabbing his servant and singing,

"Matchmaker, Matchmaker, make me a match, find me a find, catch me a catch. Night after night' my son Isaac's alone...." OK maybe the song didn't happen; but you get the idea.

The servant hears Abraham's request and thinks, *No problem.* But there is one catch: The bride can't be from Canaan. Suddenly, the job just got a lot tougher. So the servant makes a request: Instead of bringing the bride to Isaac, how about if he brings Isaac to his bride? Abraham not only refuses, he makes the servant put his hand under his thigh—a sign of submission to his master—and swear that he won't.

So not only does the servant have to convince a woman to marry a man she's never seen, he has to get her to leave her town to do it. The job seems impossible. But that's where God comes in. Abraham says that because God wants

... "Let there be light";...

Abraham's descendants in this land, somehow God will take care of it. Abraham has seen God do bigger things than that. But the servant has to make it happen, and he doesn't yet have the same faith for himself.

Here we see an example of the ripple effect of faith. Abraham gives his faith to his servant, and the servant has the opportunity to see God work for himself. The servant's first prayer asks God to work for Abraham's sake (verses 12-14). When he opens his eyes, Rebekah is standing in front of him.

When the servant prays a second time, it is no longer a third-person prayer. This prayer is now his own.

The amazing thing about this story is that the servant not only receives Abraham's faith, he passes it on. When he gets to Rebekah's house, he tells the story of how God answered his prayer. Rebekah's father and uncle respond with an affirmation of faith (verse 50). So, Rebekah packs her bags and leaves with her family's blessing.

And the servant returns with two things he didn't have before: a bride for Isaac and a faith for himself.

1. How does Abraham's faith contrast with the servant's at the beginning of the chapter?

...And there was light.

2. When do you think the servant's faith started to change?

3. Have you ever been affected by someone else's faith? If so, whose? Have you ever helped someone else become stronger in his or her faith?

Twins of Prophecy

Genesis 25

Isaac prayed to the LORD for his wife, because she was barren; and the LORD granted his prayer, and his wife Rebekah conceived. The children struggled together within her; and she said, "If it is to be this way, why do I live?" So she went to inquire of the LORD. And the LORD said to her,

And God said...

> *"Two nations are in your womb,*
> *and two peoples born of you shall be divided;*
> *the one shall be stronger than the other,*
> *the elder shall serve the younger."*
> (Genesis 25:21-23, NRSV)

There are two theories about children. One is the *nurture* theory, which says that kids develop their personalities based on their environment. The other is the *nature* theory, which says that kids' personalities are wired into them when they are born.

My best friend has four children, and she supports the nature theory. Her kids had distinct personalities from the start. She thinks that a lot of it happened before birth. My hunch is that Rebekah would have agreed.

From the start, Jacob was on Esau's heel—literally. Even as a baby, Jacob was trying to control his birth order. And he wouldn't give up until he did.

Rebekah started to feel Jacob's personality when she was pregnant. The twins jostled inside her womb. When Rebekah asked the Lord about

it, the Lord gave her a prophecy (verse 23). We can't say whether Jacob's personality was a result of the prophecy or the prophecy was a result of Jacob's personality. But God foreknew what Jacob would be like.

... "Let there be light"; ...

Esau was also a part of the prophecy. His role as firstborn would be overturned. At first, it seems unfair. But as Esau grew, it became clearer why. While Jacob was conniving, Esau was careless. This chapter gives evidence of both.

When Esau came in from hunting and asked Jacob for some food, Jacob asked for his birthright in exchange. It was a ridiculous trade, but Esau let hunger surpass his ability to think clearly. When that happens, the result is never good.

Bad decisions are made when we are overwhelmed by our desires, especially when those desires control what we do. All that mattered to Esau was getting some food, so he sold Jacob his birthright. From there, the prophecy began to unfold.

Certainly, Jacob took advantage of Esau's carelessness. But the bottom line is, Esau gave in. Neither of them knew that God had sealed their fate before birth. They made their own choices, and those choices confirmed their fate.

Is life more God's will or our choice? This chapter answers the question. Both.

...And there was light.

1. Do you think that we are more a product of our nature or environment (nurture)? Why?

2. What are the differences between Jacob's and Esau's personalities? Which one are you more like?

3. Do you feel that you make your own decisions, or do you feel that God controls everything you do? What insights do you get from this chapter, regarding this question?

Like Father, Like Son

Genesis 26

So Isaac stayed in Gerar.
When the men of that place asked him about his wife, he said,
"She is my sister," because he was afraid to say, "She is my wife."
He thought, "The men of this place might kill me on account of
Rebekah, because she is beautiful."

And
God
said ...

When Isaac had been there a long time,
Abimelech king of the Philistines looked down
from a window and saw Isaac caressing his
wife Rebekah. So Abimelech summoned Isaac
and said, "She is really your wife! Why did you
say, 'She is my sister'?"

Isaac answered him, "Because I thought I might lose my life
on account of her."

Then Abimelech said, "What is this you have done to us? One of
the men might well have slept with your wife, and you would have
brought guilt upon us." (Genesis 26:6-10, NIV)

There are some qualities we hope that we'll get from our parents; others we hope to avoid. When you hear the words, "You're just like your mother!" it can be a compliment. (Unless, of course, you're a guy). In that case, "You're just like your father!" is better, unless you've inherited some traits that aren't his best.

Isaac got some wonderful traits from Abraham. The one displayed in this chapter wasn't one of them. Isaac had inherited Abraham's fear of having a beautiful wife. Abraham could trust God in many areas, but this one he never got down. Now Isaac has his chance to trust God; but instead, he follows Abraham's lead.

At first, the story seems like déjà vu. There is an Abimelech in this story; however, it's not the same one as before, but the son or grandson of the previous king. Isaac comes to Abimelech's land at the command of God, just as his father did years ago. (see chapter 20). The same fear plagues his

... "Let
there be
light"; ...

mind as did his father's: "The men of this place might kill me on account of Rebekah, because she is beautiful" (verse 7). Sound familiar?

It makes you wonder whether Abraham told Isaac his story. But if he did, you'd think that Isaac would have learned from Abraham's mistakes. Instead, Isaac repeated the pattern: He told Abimelech that Rebekah was his sister, but eventually the truth came out.

Isaac inherited this bad trait from Abraham. But he inherited some good ones too. After he is confronted with his lie, Isaac confesses to Abimelech, and eventually Abimelech sends him away. But God gives Isaac another chance to be a witness.

Abimelech sees from afar that God's hand is on Isaac; and because of that, he comes to sign a treaty of peace (verse 28). And so, in spite of Isaac's mistake, God stays faithful to Isaac—and Isaac stays faithful to God.

And *that*, he got from his father.

1. What similarities do you see in Abraham and Isaac? What differences?

...And there was light.

2. How do you see evidence of God's commitment to Isaac in this chapter? How does it relate to God's commitment to Abraham?

3. What qualities did you get from your mother and father? Which parent are you more like?

Jacob's Blessing

Genesis 27

And God said...

So when Esau went to the field to hunt for game and bring it, Rebekah said to her son Jacob, "I heard your father say to your brother Esau, "Bring me game, and prepare for me savory food to eat, that I may bless you before the LORD before I die.' Now therefore, my son, obey my word as I command you. Go to the flock, and get me two choice kids, so that I may prepare from them savory food for your father, such as he likes; and you shall take it to your father to eat, so that he may bless you before he dies."
(Genesis 27:5b-10, NRSV)

Imagine that it's Christmas morning, and you're excited to open your presents—especially the one from your dad. All week you've looked at the box under the tree with your name on it. You can't wait to see what it is. So you make your dad his favorite breakfast, take it in on a tray, when suddenly you turn the corner and you can't believe your eyes. Your brother has opened your gift!

Horrified, you look at your mother only to find that she was the one who gave it to him! In desperation, you turn to your father convinced that he will make it all right. Instead, he looks down and says helplessly, "Your brother got here first. The present is his now."

Then you wake up from your nightmare. At least, you hope you do. I'm sure that's what

Esau wanted to do in this chapter. But for him, it wasn't a dream. It was how Jacob ended up with his blessing.

God uses imperfect people to accomplish God's purposes. This story is an example of that. Rebekah had received

... "Let there be light"; ...

God's prophecy about Jacob and Esau, and she was waiting for it to be fulfilled. She knew that Isaac was about to give his blessing to Esau, so she intervened and sent Jacob in Esau's place. She probably felt that she was fulfilling God's will, but the way she did it was questionable—at best.

Jacob is a bit more innocent than Rebekah is in this chapter, but he was a prime player in

64

the deceit. He wasn't concerned about his brother's feelings. The only concern he had was that he might get caught (verse 12). Jacob may have felt justified in his actions because Esau had already sold him his birthright. But Jacob's motives were mixed—at best.

Esau is the victim in this story, but a closer look helps you see his part. By giving his birthright to Jacob for some soup, he revealed how little he cared for it. Now he cried when it was taken away. If Esau had a stronger character, perhaps the story would have been different; but Esau was weak and vulnerable—at best.

And so the promise is fulfilled: The younger son will rule over the elder. The way God's will unfolds is messy. Yet in God's sovereign plan we trust it was best.

1. Do you think that Jacob and Rebekah should have done what they did to get Isaac's blessing? Why, or why not?

...And there was light.

2. Do you think that God knew everything that would happen in this chapter? If so, do you think that God approved?

3. If God knows all of the decisions that you will make, are you really making them? Why, or why not?

A Vision and a Promise

Genesis 28

Jacob left Beer-sheba and went toward Haran. He came to a certain place and stayed there for the night, because the sun had set. Taking one of the stones of the place, he put it under his head and lay down in that place. And he dreamed that there was a ladder set up on the earth, the top of it reaching to heaven; and

And God said ...

the angels of God were ascending and descending on it. And the LORD stood beside him and said, "I am the LORD, the God of Abraham your father and the God of Isaac; the land on which you lie I will give to you and to your offspring.
(Genesis 28:10-13, NRSV)

Have you ever had a dream so real that you thought that it had actually happened? If it's a bad dream, you wake up feeling relieved; but if it's a good dream, you want to go back to sleep—or at least find a way to remember it. That's what Jacob did in this chapter.

After the turmoil in the last chapter, Jacob is separated from his family and on his way to a land he's never been. As he lies down to sleep, I can only imagine his feelings: concern over his brother, sadness over his mother and father, fear over what lies ahead. But most of all, I imagine that Jacob feels very alone—until he is met by God in a dream.

Up to this point, Jacob has had little faith. His tendency has been to do things for himself. However, Jacob is changed by this dream. He

knows he is not by himself anymore. While Jacob's eyes were closed in sleep, he saw what he couldn't see when he was awake. The door between heaven and earth opened up, and Jacob could see God. And this vision stayed with him when he woke up.

... "Let there be light"; ...

When we see God, we don't forget it; it makes an impression on our hearts. Whether it's a dream or a conversation, an experience or a sign, God reaches out to us in many ways. Usually it's very personal, something meant just for us. For Jacob, it was a message to reassure him that God was with him. God gave him the same promise that his father and grandfather had received. No longer did Jacob have to rely on their stories for his faith. Now he had a story of his own.

Jacob's response to God shows that his faith was progressive. He starts with a conditional vow. He says, "*If God will be with me, . . . then the* LORD *shall be my God*" (verses 20-21). Many of us do the same thing. We pray, "If you'll do this, God, then I'll believe." As we mature, our prayers change. But God is willing to meet us right where we are.

That's how God met Jacob. It all started with a vision in a dream. God will continue to work on Jacob—his strengths and weaknesses will be tested and tried. But Jacob knows now that God is with him, so he won't have to face his challenges alone.

Jacob's dream ended when he woke up. But his new life had just begun.

1. What was the last dream you had that you remember? Why do you remember it?

...And there was light.

2. How do you think Jacob was different after his dream? Have you ever felt different after you woke up from a dream?

3. If God were to communicate to you through a vision or a sign, what do you think God would say to you? Why?

But when evening came, he took his daughter Leah and gave her to Jacob, and Jacob lay with her. And Laban gave his servant girl Zilpah to his daughter as her maidservant.

When morning came, there was Leah! So Jacob said to Laban, "What is this you have done to me? I served you for Rachel, didn't I? Why have you deceived me?"

And God said...

Laban replied, "It is not our custom here to give the younger daughter in marriage before the older one. Finish this daughter's bridal week; then we will give you the younger one also, in return for another seven years of work."
(Genesis 29:23-27, NIV)

God loves us as we are—but too much to let us stay that way. That's what Jacob is finding out. We all have areas of our lives that God wants to work on, and God uses our circumstances to show us what those areas are.

Just two chapters ago, Jacob cheated Esau out of his blessing. Now Jacob's father-in-law has done the same thing to him. For seven years, Jacob works for Laban in order to marry Laban's daughter Rachel. But Laban tricks him and gives him Leah instead. Jacob wakes up to find the woman he thought he had married was not the woman in his bed. Instead of his familiar role as deceiver, Jacob was the one deceived. Now he had the opportunity to feel what others had felt because of him.

God uses the circumstances in our lives to show us where we need to grow. Our journey here is not just what happens *to* us; it's what happens *in* us. That's what concerns God most. Jacob needed to learn humility and patience, so God allowed

..."Let there be light";...

his circumstances to teach him just that. Up until this point, Jacob has controlled his destiny and disregarded others to get what he wants. Now Jacob has lost control of his destiny, and he has to accommodate others to get what he deserves.

Jacob has to work seven more years for the bride he wants, while staying married to the bride he has. In the meantime, he acquires two more brides. It's not the love story Jacob dreamed of, but it's the one God will use in his life. With four women, Jacob will have to learn patience; and his conniving nature will undoubtedly be outmatched.

God doesn't always fix our circumstances, but God can use our circumstances to fix us. When we view our lives from this perspective, we're less concerned with what happens to us and more concerned with how we respond. That's the definition of spiritual growth.

Jacob couldn't control his circumstances, but he could learn to control himself. That's what God wants for all of us. So the next time you face circumstances you don't want, remember Jacob. They might just be the circumstances you need.

...And there was light.

1. What circumstances in your life frustrate you most right now? Why?

2. Do you think that God has ever allowed certain circumstances into your life for a reason? What do you think the reason was?

3. What qualities did God need to work on in Jacob? What qualities does God need to work on in you?

Leah and Rachel

Genesis 30

When Rachel saw that she bore Jacob no children, she envied her sister; and she said to Jacob, "Give me children, or I shall die!" Jacob became very angry with Rachel and said, "Am I in the place of God, who has withheld from you the fruit of the womb? ... "

And God said ...

In the days of wheat harvest Reuben went and found mandrakes in the field, and brought them to his mother Leah. Then Rachel said to Leah, "Please give me some of your son's mandrakes." But she said to her, "Is it a small matter that you have taken away my husband? Would you take away my son's mandrakes also?" Rachel said, "Then he may lie with you tonight for your son's mandrakes."
(Genesis 30:1-2, 14-15, NRSV)

Imagine that your sister is getting married, but your father has decided to put you in her place. The bridegroom wouldn't find out until it was too late—when he woke up to find you in his bed. The moment you dreamed of all your life is about to turn into a nightmare, with you as the star. That's what happened to Leah.

Now imagine you are Leah's sister. A man came into your life, and you fell in love. He offered to work for your father for seven years to win you as his bride. For seven long years, you wait, long for, and dream of the day this marriage will come to pass. But your father informs you the day of the wedding that your sister will be taking your place. That's what happened to Rachel.

Both Leah and Rachel experienced loss and heartbreak, but neither were forgotten by God. Leah watched her sister have her husband's heart. Rachel watched her sister have her husband's sons. And God observed the pain of both. Neither woman had everything she wanted, but both

... "Let there be light"; ...

women experienced God's grace.

They were humbled by their circumstances. While Leah had to bargain for Jacob's affection (verse 15), Rachel had to bargain for Jacob's seed (verse 1). But they were also honored in their circumstances. Leah was blessed with her fertility, and Rachel was blessed with her husband's love. Leah never had as much love, and Rachel never had as many children;

but both had a measure of God's blessing. This shows us how God works in our lives.

Life is filled with blessings and challenges, and God wants us to learn to live with both. In Philippians 4:12, Paul says that he has learned "the secret of being content in any and every situation, whether well fed or hungry, whether living in plenty or in want" (NIV). According to Paul, we get to determine whether we'll live bitterly or gratefully. Will we focus on the things we don't have? Or will we look at the things we do have?

Paul may give us the answer. But our lives give us the opportunity.

...And there was light.

1. Make a list of all the blessings and challenges that God has given you. Which are harder for you to think of?

2. In your opinion, who had the greatest challenge, Rachel or Leah? Who had the greatest blessing?

3. Do you tend to focus on your blessings or your challenges? How does Philippians 4:12 encourage you in your perspective?

The Cycle of Deceit

Genesis 31

Then the LORD said to Jacob, "Return to the land of your ancestors and to your kindred, and I will be with you...."
Then Rachel and Leah answered him, "Is there any portion or inheritance left to us in our father's house? Are we not regarded by him as foreigners? For he has sold us, and he has been using up the money given for us. All the property that God has taken away from our father belongs to us and to our children; now then, do whatever God has said to you."
(Genesis 31:3, 14-16, NRSV)

And God said...

Have you ever heard the saying "What goes around, comes around?" That's an accurate phrase to describe Laban in this chapter. That is, until God breaks through.

As the father of Leah and Rachel, Laban had deceived Jacob so that he would end up marrying them both. Laban had discounted the desires of his daughters and made all of their decisions for personal gain. For a while, it seemed that Laban benefited from his deceit: Jacob worked for him for fourteen years, his children and grandchildren surrounded him, and he seemed to prosper undeservedly. But time eventually presented to Laban the consequences of his actions.

Jacob may have been deceived by Laban, but he knew the game well enough to fight back. When Laban made Jacob stay and work, Jacob began breeding strong animals with spotted ones, to develop the strongest flocks for himself. Then Jacob tells his wives of his plans to leave, and they tell Jacob that they'll go with him. They have no loyalty to their

..."Let there be light";...

father, because he has shown no loyalty to them. Off they run, with no goodbye. And Laban is left with the consequences of poor parenting.

Galatians 6:7b says, "You reap whatever you sow." In this chapter, we see that it's true. Laban deceived others to get what he wanted; and ultimately, he was deceived. He passed a legacy of deceit onto his children, and they ended up being deceivers too. They snuck off and left their father, paying him back for all the times he had mistreated them.

The good news is that even in the cycle of deceit, God can break through to heal and restore. Laban sets out to seek revenge on Jacob, when he is met by God in a dream. God's words to Laban stop him from harming Jacob and they end up forming a covenant. Laban kisses his daughters and grandchildren goodbye, allowing them to begin their own lives. It's Laban's last scene in the Bible, and it is his best. He listened to God and broke the cycle of deceit.

God has the power to break cycles, but we have to let God break us first. Laban did that in this chapter.

Jacob will have his chance next.

1. Do you think that Laban was a good father? Why, or why not?

...And there was light.

2. How did Laban change in this chapter? What caused him to change? What effect do you think it had on his family?

3. If God wanted to change a negative pattern in your family, what would it be? Is there anything you could do to start that change?

Wrestling With God

Genesis 32

Jacob was left alone; and a man wrestled with him until daybreak. When the man saw that he did not prevail against Jacob, he struck him on the hip socket; and Jacob's hip was put out of joint as he wrestled with him. Then he said, "Let me go, for the day is breaking." But Jacob said, "I will not let you go, unless you bless me." So he said to him, "What is your name?" And he said, "Jacob." Then the man said, "You shall no longer be called Jacob, but Israel, for you have striven with God and with humans, and have prevailed."
(Genesis 32:24-28, NRSV)

And God said...

Several years ago in Paris, I sat in a church, staring at a huge painting of a man and an angel locked in a wrestling match. It was an artist's rendering of this chapter. In the painting, Jacob's face was buried in the chest of this huge winged creature nearly twice his size. The angel's face was focused on Jacob's head, and he seemed to be trying to get Jacob to look up. The angel was trying to lessen the struggle and lead him in a dance. The angel was so much bigger and more powerful than Jacob that he could have overpowered him in an instant. But he had a gentle expression on his face that seemed to indicate that he was going to let Jacob have it out with him. And he would stay with him until the struggle was through.

That painting has become an image to me of what it's like to try to control God. Jacob struggled with this his whole life—first tricking Esau out of his blessing, then tricking Laban out of his flocks. Jacob was constantly taking things into his own hands; but, in the last chapter, Jacob experienced God's intervention. God had protected Jacob by meeting Laban in a dream (31:29). Finally, Jacob had been given the opportunity to experience God's power without his own intervention.

..."Let there be light";...

Now Jacob is about to face Esau. He knows that this will be the struggle of his life. He deceived Esau and stole his birthright, and they have not seen each other since. Jacob prepares for their meeting in the usual way: sending gifts to bribe Esau and dividing his goods to protect himself. Then he calls on God to support him (verse 11). Jacob learns at the end of this chapter that God is more than a support to his strategies. God is the one in control.

After Jacob sends his presents, his servants, and his family ahead of him, he is finally all alone. An angel appears in the form of a man, and the two of them wrestle until daybreak. The angel starts to leave; but Jacob grasps him, saying, "I will not let you go, unless you bless me" (verse 26). Jacob has spent his life trying to acquire his blessings himself; now he finally realizes who the source of blessing really is.

Jacob gets his blessing, but he is also left with a wound. From now on, Jacob will limp to remind him of his dependence on God. And that was the blessing Jacob needed most.

1. How did Jacob change after he wrestled with God? Do you think that Jacob became stronger or weaker than he was before? Why?

...And there was light.

2. Have you ever "wrestled with God" about something? If so, what was it?

3. What might God "break" in you if God were to wrestle you? How would it change you?

Surprised by Grace

Genesis 33

He put the maids with their children in front, then Leah with her children, and Rachel and Joseph last of all. He himself went on ahead of them, bowing himself to the ground seven times, until he came near his brother.
But Esau ran to meet him, and embraced him, and fell on his neck and kissed him, and they wept.
(Genesis 33:2-4, NRSV)

 And God said...

If anyone had a right to be angry, it was Esau. Twenty years ago, Jacob stole Esau's birthright and left him to pick up the pieces of a life he neither wanted nor deserved. Thanks to Jacob, Esau had a strained relationship with his father and mother and had to deal with the effects of Jacob's trickery all alone. Now, twenty years later, Jacob and Esau were about to meet for the very first time. You can only imagine how Jacob felt.

It's a little like how you might feel when you know you've done something wrong and your parents are on their way home. Suddenly, you start cleaning the kitchen and mowing the lawn and doing every chore you can think of. Your hope is that a trimmed lawn and a clean kitchen will

soften them up. That way they might spare your life.

Jacob had those same thoughts about facing Esau; and the gifts he sent ahead were an attempt to lessen the blow. While Esau is still far off, Jacob begins bowing in ..."Let there be light";... humility and fear. Suddenly, in an act of sheer grace, Esau runs to Jacob, throws his arms around him and kisses him. I can only imagine Jacob's shock. What he expected was judgment and condemnation. What he got, instead, was grace. It was an Old Testament version of the prodigal son (Luke 15). This may have even been the story Jesus thought

76

about when he told that parable. Like the father of the prodigal, Esau welcomes Jacob with undeserved grace. And Jacob witnesses the presence of God (verse 10).

That's what happens when we forgive others who don't deserve it. It takes a strength outside ourselves. Esau had to find that strength early on to make it through his circumstances. Otherwise, he would have been swallowed up by bitterness. Ironically, when we choose bitterness over forgiveness, we are the ones who suffer—even if our bitterness is justifiable. Conversely, when we choose to forgive when others do not deserve it, we are the ones who are free.

Even though Jacob stole Esau's blessing, God took care of Esau (verse 9). Therefore, Esau doesn't need for Jacob to pay him back. It is an example to us of what grace can do—not only in the lives of those we forgive, but in our own lives. When we let God take care of our injustice, we can experience the surprise of grace.

1. How would you have felt toward Jacob if you were Esau? Could you have responded the way Esau did? Why, or why not?

...And there was light.

2. Is there anyone in your life you feel resentment toward? How have you handled it?

3. How does this chapter encourage you in your relationships with people who have hurt you? Is there someone in your life you need to forgive? If so, will you be able to?

Results of Revenge

Genesis 34

The sons of Jacob answered Shechem and his father Hamor deceitfully, because he had defiled their sister Dinah. They said to them, "We cannot do this thing, to give our sister to one who is uncircumcised, for that would be a disgrace to us. Only on this condition will we consent to you: that you will become as we are

And God said ...

and every male among you be circumcised. Then we will give our daughters to you, and we will take your daughters for ourselves, and we will live among you and become one people....

And all who went out of the city gate heeded Hamor and his son Shechem; and every male was circumcised, all who went out of the gate of his city.

On the third day, when they were still in pain, two of the sons of Jacob, Simeon and Levi, Dinah's brothers, took their swords and came against the city unawares, and killed all the males. (Genesis 34:13-16, 24-25, NRSV)

This chapter stands in stark contrast to the one that precedes it, and it illustrates the consequences of revenge. While grace brings out the best in us; revenge brings out the worst in us. We are never more unlike God than when we are plotting to get someone back.

Maybe you've been in that situation with some friends: They've hurt you, and you want to hurt them too. It's a natural human response, but it's not a God response. And nobody wins in the end—this story illustrates that fact.

Jacob's daughter, Dinah, has wandered into town to visit the women of the land. She is met by Shechem, the son of Hamor; and verse 2 says that he "he took her and violated her." (NIV) Shechem doesn't just use Dinah as a prostitute, he

wants to marry her (verse 4); but Dinah's brothers are so filled with bitterness and hatred over her violation, they are consumed with the need for revenge.

This sets the stage for what happens next.

Simeon and Levi lie

... "Let there be light"; ...

to Shechem and tell him that if he and all the males in the city get circumcised, he will be able to marry their sister. It speaks of Shechem's commitment to Dinah that he and the men agree to this; but after they do, Simeon and Levi come in and murder them. It's a punishment that far outweighs the crime, and a testimony to the results of revenge. By focusing on their hatred, Simeon and Levi spread it around; and what started as a terrible offense soon became a full blown war.

It's the opposite of what Esau did in the previous chapter. Instead of focusing on Jacob's wrongdoing, he trusted God with it and let it go. And God eventually replaced his bitterness with grace.

That's not what happened to Simeon and Levi. Their enemies weren't the only ones who suffered. Ultimately, they did too. They were not honored by their father for their actions. They were criticized for being a disgrace. And *disgrace* is the perfect word to end this chapter.

1. How does this chapter compare to or contrast with the previous chapter? Which one reflects God more?

...And there was light.

2. Have you ever wanted to take revenge on someone? If so, how did you handle it?

3. Do you think that Simeon and Levi regretted their behavior? Why, or why not? What can you learn from their actions?

God's Timing

Then they journeyed from Bethel; and when they were still some distance from Ephrath, Rachel was in childbirth, and she had hard labor. When she was in her hard labor, the midwife said to her, "Do not be afraid; for now you will have another son." As her soul was departing (for she died), she named him Ben-oni; but his father called him Benjamin. So Rachel died, and she was buried on the way to Ephrath (that is, Bethlehem).
(Genesis 35:16-19, NRSV)

And God said...

All her married life, Rachel longed to have more children. Her sister had given birth to six sons, and Rachel had given birth to one. I'm sure that she cried to God many times for a second child. But this chapter shows why God held back.

The child Rachel longed for would end her earthly life. If she had given birth to Benjamin in her own timing, she would have died long before. Instead, she gave birth in God's timing; and her life was extended by God's grace. I'm sure Rachel didn't view it as grace when Leah had so many children while she had only one. But God knew that Rachel's second birth would cause her death, so the delay had extended her life.

In Genesis 30:24, after Rachel had just given birth to Joseph, she prayed, "May the Lord add to me another son." God waited many years to answer that prayer. In the meantime, she could be a mother to the son she already had.

So often, we don't understand why God chooses not to answer certain prayers; but time often reveals why God holds  **..."Let there be light";...** back. Can you think of a prayer that God didn't answer the way you wanted? If not, someday you will. And the choice we have as Christians is how to handle it when it happens.

When we believe that God is out for our good, even when it feels bad, we can trust that God is caring for us. The alternative is rejecting God's plan—and we miss seeing the story unfold.

Many people do reject God, and their story ends prematurely with heartache and disappointment. However, that is never how it ends with God. In time, heartache and disappointment always turn to joy. But we have to see the story through.

Rachel had her second son, but she died the day he was born. God's grace in holding back Benjamin's birth allowed Rachel to be a mother to Joseph so that he could pass along her memory to his brother. Rachel died holding the answer to her prayer.

Nevertheless, Rachel's death is still not the end of the story. With God, it has only begun.

1. How do you think Rachel felt when God delayed answering her prayer? Have you ever felt that way?

...And there was light.

2. What evidence of God's grace do you see in the timing of the birth of Rachel's second son? Do you think that it felt like grace to Rachel? to Jacob?

3. What lesson does this chapter teach us about unanswered prayers? How can it help you when you have a prayer that remains unanswered?

Esau Remembered

Genesis 36

Then Esau took his wives, his sons, his daughters, and all the members of his household, his cattle, all his livestock, and all the property he had acquired in the land of Canaan; and he moved to a land some distance from his brother Jacob. For their possessions were too great for them to live together; the land where they were staying could not support them because of their livestock. So Esau settled in the hill country of Seir; Esau is Edom.
(Genesis 36:6-8, NRSV)

And God said ...

After setting such an example of grace, it is fitting that Esau should have a chapter dedicated to his lineage. But if you're like me, you are tempted to skim it. However, it's only when we look carefully that we see evidence of God's sovereign care for Esau. And after all Esau went through, I think it's worth a closer look.

The first evidence of God's blessing on Esau's life comes in verse 7. The combined possessions of Jacob and Esau were too great for them to remain together; and the land where they were staying couldn't support them both. So, the reason Esau settled in another land was because of *blessing*, not banishment. God had blessed Jacob and Esau equally with family, livestock, and goods; and they had to separate to have enough space.

Because of their renewed relationship (thanks to Esau), they separated amicably. And Esau settled in the country of Seir.

Another interesting detail of this chapter is that one of Esau's wives was Basemath, the daughter of Ishmael. Ishmael and Esau were the older brothers of Isaac and Jacob; and both had experienced their younger brother being the recipient of God's blessing. God binds them together in their lineage and they are both promised God's care, in spite of the fact that they didn't receive the blessing. The joining of their families under Esau's prosperity shows

... "Let there be light"; ...

God's promise to be true.

Verse 15 mentions there are "chiefs" among Esau's descendants, a clear statement of the importance of Esau's clan, the Edomites. Although they were not the chosen Israelites, the Edomites had a prominent place in the development and structure of society, showing that they were not forgotten by God.

One last interesting fact in this lineage is that one of Esau's sons was named Eliphaz, who had a son named Teman. In the Book of Job, Eliphaz the Temanite was listed as one of Job's friends (Job 2:11). This raises the possibility of connection between Job and the Edomites. The story of Job gives us the message that we must hold fast to God's goodness, even when our circumstances seem to deny it. In the end, God always comes through.

Esau found that out first. This chapter shows us how.

1. What similarities do you see between Esau and Ishmael? What differences do you see?

...And there was light.

2. Why do you think there is a whole chapter devoted to Esau's lineage? What does that tell you about Esau?

3. What do you think would have happened to Esau if he never forgave Jacob? What lesson does that teach you about forgiveness?

Divine Dreams

Genesis 37

Once Joseph had a dream, and when he told it to his brothers, they hated him even more. He said to them, "Listen to this dream that I dreamed. There we were, binding sheaves in the field. Suddenly my sheaf rose and stood upright; then your sheaves gathered around it, and bowed down to my sheaf." His brothers said to him, "Are you indeed to reign over us? Are you indeed to have dominion over us?" So they hated him even more because of his dreams and his words. (Genesis 37:5-8, NRSV)

And God said...

Have you ever had a dream that was so real that you just had to tell someone about it? That's what happened to Joseph. The problem was, he didn't think it through first.

When you have a dream that involves someone else, you have to be careful how you talk about it—especially if something bad happens. Joseph's dreams revealed that one day everyone in his family would bow to him. Obviously, this wasn't going to be good news for his brothers. They were already jealous of him because he had been given a special robe. If Joseph had been more thoughtful, he would have kept his dream to himself. But Joseph's naive arrogance led him to tell it with exuberance.

You can imagine their response. What would you do if your little brother told you about a dream like that? Let's hope that you'd be a little easier on him than Joseph's brothers were. They decided to kill him and throw him into a cistern! Reuben, who was the eldest and most compassionate, convinced the brothers not to kill Joseph. Eventually, Joseph's brothers rethought their actions and sold him as a slave, instead.

... "Let there be light"; ...

At every juncture in Joseph's story, God is at work in the bigger picture of his life. Joseph's dreams were a picture of the ultimate future God had in mind for him, but he needed to go through a few things first.

The naive arrogance that characterized Joseph's early

years will eventually be chipped away, and God will humble him to make that happen. If you were bound by your brothers, thrown into a cistern, and sold as a slave it might cause you to rethink the way you've handled your relationship with them. Obviously, Joseph's brothers' were wrong; but they were provoked by Joseph's egotism. And it was that egotism that needed work.

So God allowed Joseph to be humbled, but Joseph wasn't left alone. God would continue to be with Joseph, but his journey toward being a ruler would begin as a humble slave.

And only God could pave a journey like that.

1. Do you think that Joseph should have told his brothers about his dream? Why, or why not?

...And there was light.

2. Have you ever had a dream where something good happened to you that was bad for someone else? If you had that kind of dream, would you tell anyone about it?

3. How would you respond if someone told you that he or she was destined to be greater than you? Would you be happy for that person—or jealous of him or her?

Tamar's Tenacity

Genesis 38

About three months later Judah was told, "Your daughter-in-law Tamar is guilty of prostitution, and as a result she is now pregnant."

Judah said, "Bring her out and have her burned to death!"

As she was being brought out, she sent a message to her father-in-law.  *"I am pregnant by the man who owns these," she* And God said... *said. And she added, "See if you recognize whose seal and cord and staff these are." Judah recognized them and said, "She is more righteous than I, since I wouldn't give her to my son Shelah." And he did not sleep with her again.*

(Genesis 38:24-26, NIV)

In this chapter, we take a break from Joseph's story to follow the line of Judah. It seems like an abrupt interruption; however, Judah is part of the genealogy of Christ (see Matthew 1). Therefore, it's important for us to know his story.

Judah's story is not a heroic one. But this chapter focuses on Judah's daughter-in-law, Tamar, and her determination to see justice prevail. It's because of her that things happened the way they did, although her actions were questionable. But God must have understood her desperation; because those actions secured her place as one of five women mentioned in the lineage of Christ (Matthew 1:3).

The first observation we make is that Judah left his brothers and settled by himself among the Canaanites (verse 1).

When we separate ourselves from fellow believers, we put ourselves in jeopardy, because we are influenced by the company we keep. This certainly happened to Judah and his family.

Tamar is first mentioned as the wife Judah ... "Let there be light"; ... got for Er, his firstborn son. We don't know what Er did to make God angry, but it was wicked enough to be put to death (verse 7). Tamar is then given to Onan, Judah's second son, and he too is put to death. The result of both sons' wickedness is that Tamar was left widowed and childless through no fault of her own.

Judah had promised Tamar his third son, Shelah, but he

doesn't give him to her. This paved the way for Tamar to make things happen on her own.

Judah's wife died, and he decided to take a trip to Timnah; and this is when Tamar saw her opportunity. She covered her face with a veil and posed as a prostitute along the street. Judah slept with her, and three months later, it is discovered that Tamar is pregnant. She is sentenced to death until the shocking truth is revealed that Judah is the father. Because Judah realizes why Tamar did what she did, she is forgiven and commended. He never sleeps with her again.

Tamar has her sons; and she becomes part of the genealogy of Christ. It's an amazing story that proves that we have a God who can take our sinful plan and weave together a sovereign plan. And only a big God can do that.

1. Do you think that what Tamar did in this chapter was right? Why, or why not?

...And there was light.

2. What strengths and weaknesses do you see in Tamar? What strengths and weaknesses do you see in Judah?

3. What does this chapter teach you about God's grace? How can you apply what you've learned to your own need for grace?

Joseph and Potiphar's Wife

Genesis 39

So he left all that he had in Joseph's charge; and, with him there, he had no concern for anything but the food that he ate.
Now Joseph was handsome and good-looking. And after a time his master's wife cast her eyes on Joseph and said, "Lie with me."
But he refused and said to his master's wife, "Look, with me here, my master has no concern about anything in the house,

And God said . . .

and he has put everything that he has in my hand. He is not greater in this house than I am, nor has he kept back anything from me except yourself, because you are his wife. How then could I do this great wickedness, and sin against God?" And although she spoke to Joseph day after day, he would not consent to lie beside her or to be with her.
(Genesis 39:6-10, NRSV)

This chapter could be called "Desperate Housewife." Under the pressure of that theme, Joseph has his first chance to shine. Anyone who struggles with temptation will never have a struggle bigger than Joseph had. And his response shows us how to make it through.

Notice the subtle approach of Potiphar's wife (verse 7). Not many men get that kind of invitation. I'm sure that it was difficult to pass up. However, Joseph's response gives us the first lesson on avoiding temptation: Reaffirm the reasons why you shouldn't give in. This is hard to do when you are in the midst of temptation. Let's face it, when your hormones are hopping it's hard to think clearly about anything. That's what gets us into trouble.

Instead of thinking about what we should do, we tend to rationalize what we want to do. And that's where we can learn from Joseph. One by one, he reaffirms the reasons why he shouldn't have sex with Potiphar's wife: First, her husband was the one who put him in charge. What a betrayal

. . . "Let there be light"; . . .

that would be! Second, nothing had been withheld from Joseph, except *her*. (If only Adam and Eve had used this strategy in the garden). Third, if Joseph does this, he will not only sin against Potiphar, he will sin against God.

Listing your reasons for not giving in to temptation strengthens your resolve. And Joseph needed that strength for what was to come.

Potiphar's wife spoke to him day after day. Can you imagine the strength that took? Every day he had to face the same temptation, and every day he had to say no. Finally, she became so desperate that she grabbed his cloak and said, "Come to bed with me!"

Now Joseph is naked (or close to it) and a beautiful woman stands in front of him. So he does what any respectable man would do at that point. Run!

When temptation gets so great that you can't stand up to it, you always have the option to run. Sometimes that's what it takes. Joseph passed his test with flying colors, but the apparent injustice of God is that he ends up in jail for doing the right thing.

But remember that word *apparent*. God's got Joseph's back.

1. What is the biggest temptation you've ever faced? Are you still dealing with it?

...And there was light.

2. Do you think that you could be as strong as Joseph was in this chapter? Why, or why not?

3. What's the greatest lesson you got out of this chapter about resisting temptation? How can you apply it to your life?

Trust in Trials

Genesis 40

"Within three days Pharaoh will lift up your head and restore you to your office; and you shall place Pharaoh's cup in his hand, just as you used to do when you were his cupbearer. But remember me when it is well with you; please do me the kindness to make mention of me to Pharaoh, and so get me out of this place. For in fact I was stolen out of the land of the Hebrews; and here also I have done nothing that they should have put me into the dungeon...."

And God said...

Yet the chief cupbearer did not remember Joseph, but forgot him.
(Genesis 40:13-15, 23, NRSV)

Have you ever felt forgotten by God? If so, this is the chapter for you. It definitely represents the low point of Joseph's journey. As you read it, you'll see why.

The last chapter ends with Joseph being punished for a crime he did not commit. Now he was sitting in jail. Joseph could easily have wallowed in his bitterness. It would have been hard not to.

Lesson 1 for making it through a trial is to *trust God.* Even if everything around you seems unfair and wrong, hang on to God! It's when we let go that we mess things up. Sometimes God is working in a way that far surpasses our understanding. That's what was happening to Joseph. From his perspective, he was abused and forgotten. But from God's perspective, he was right where he needed to be. Jail was the road that would lead Joseph to the palace. But Joseph couldn't see it yet.

Sometimes we experience heartbreak and disappointment, and it feels as though God has let us down. But down the road,

... "Let there be light"; ...

we have a different perspective. Have you ever prayed for something God didn't give you that later you were glad you didn't get? Sometimes we have to trust that God knows more than we know. And that takes a very big faith.

Lesson 2 for making it through a trial is to *keep doing the right thing.* Never are we more tempted to sin than when we feel that God doesn't care.

I'm sure that was how Joseph felt. Yet in spite of how he felt, it was how he acted that made the difference. He earned the trust of the jailer. He became head of the jail. When the cupbearer and the baker had troubling dreams, he offered to interpret them. By continuing to do the right thing, Joseph was setting himself up to be in the right place. Eventually, his actions would pay off.

Joseph's interpretations of the cupbearer and baker's dreams were true. The cupbearer was reinstated to his position, and Joseph told him to remember him when he got to the palace (verse 14). But the cupbearer did not remember Joseph; he forgot him. And once again, Joseph had to trust.

You see, God was writing Joseph's story. And he would be remembered when the timing was right.

1. Why is it hard to trust God in the midst of a trial? Do you think that it was hard for Joseph to do so?

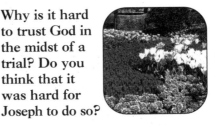

...And there was light.

2. Have you ever felt forgotten by God? If so, how did you handle it? After reading this chapter, do you think that you would handle it differently if it were to happen again?

3. What lessons do you learn from this chapter about God's plan and timing? How can these lessons help you in your life right now?

Perseverance Pays Off

Genesis 41

After two whole years, Pharaoh dreamed that he was standing by the Nile....

Then Pharaoh sent for Joseph, and he was hurriedly brought out of the dungeon. When he had shaved himself and changed his clothes, he came in before Pharaoh....

The proposal pleased Pharaoh and all his servants. **And God said ...** *Pharaoh said to his servants, "Can we find anyone else like this—one in whom is the spirit of God?"* (Genesis 41:1, 14, 37-38, NRSV)

After two whole years.

Those are the first four words of this chapter. Often we brush by these kinds of statements and jump into the next scene. But I want to pause here for a minute. That means that Joseph sat in jail for two full years. Can you imagine how he felt? Probably the same way we feel when God seems to have abandoned us. But God's timing is not our timing. God is at work far beyond our immediate view.

Throughout our lives, we go through times of waiting before we experience the unfolding of God's plan. The question is, why? As we learned through Abraham and Sarah's journey, God works on our faith while we wait. Our part is how we respond. Joseph could have become bitter toward God during this time and rejected his faith. Many people do. Instead, Joseph persevered and continued to trust even when God was not doing what he wanted. And he got to watch how God came through.

After two years, Pharaoh had a dream; and the cupbearer  ..."Let there be light"; ... finally remembered Joseph. So Joseph was brought to the palace to interpret Pharaoh's dream. Pharaoh was so impressed with Joseph's interpretation that he quickly made him head of the palace, second only to himself. In an instant, all those years of confusion and waiting were over. But it was Joseph's faithfulness along the way that brought him to this point.

How many times Joseph must have questioned his journey. If he had tried to interpret what was going on at any given moment, he would have been left with hopelessness and despair. He might have ended his life or, at the very least, thrown out his faith. The dream of becoming greater than all his brothers was a distant memory. Yet, here he finally was, seeing his dream come true.

Joseph was a different man now; the prideful arrogance of his youth had been replaced by humility, and strength. It was all part of God's plan. We finally see what Joseph's journey has produced.

God allows us to go through times of suffering because our character is more important than our comfort. We are on this earth not only to do God's will, but to become God's people—and suffering and endurance are what shape us most.

Just ask Joseph.

1. How do you think Joseph was changed by his time spent in jail? Do you think that it made him better or worse? Why?

...And there was light.

2. What similarities do you see between the way Joseph acted in jail and the way he acted in Pharaoh's palace? What does this tell you about Joseph?

3. Would you describe this time in your life as more like Joseph in jail or Joseph in the palace? Why?

Unrecognized Reunion

Genesis 42

Now Joseph was the governor of the land, the one who sold grain to all its people. So when Joseph's brothers arrived, they bowed down to him with their faces to the ground. As soon as Joseph saw his brothers, he recognized them, but he pretended to be a stranger and spoke harshly to them. "Where do you come from?" he asked.

"From the land of Canaan," they replied, "to buy food."

And God said... *Although Joseph recognized his brothers, they did not recognize him. Then he remembered his dreams about them and said to them, "You are spies! You have come to see where our land is unprotected."*

(Genesis 42:6-9, NIV)

It's hard to imagine the emotions Joseph felt when he saw his brothers come to the door. I could imagine a wave of elation ...then sadness ...then anger. But it was anger that came through when he initially spoke (verse 7). The powerful leader Joseph had suddenly reverted to the little brother who was scorned years ago. And that's not unusual when someone comes face to face with his past.

My mother (who is a therapist) calls it "confronting your inner child." It's the part of us that surfaces when we're propelled into our past. Sometimes it happens through a familiar emotion that you felt as a child. Other times, it's through a familiar person who comes back into your life. For Joseph, it was a combination of both.

Verse seven says that "As soon as Joseph saw his brothers, he recognized them"; but it was clear that they didn't know who he was. It was probably because of his Egyptian influence. (He undoubtedly had a lot less hair.)

... "Let there be light"; ...

The brothers bowed in humility to his authority; and Joseph was finally able to see his childhood dream come to pass.

All of these things must have brought to the surface many emotions in Joseph; because we see those emotions in how he behaved. First, he is angry, accusing them of being spies.

Then he puts them in prison. Finally, he insists on seeing their youngest brother. It all makes sense to us as we read the story; but it must have been very confusing for Joseph's brothers. They wonder why they're being treated this way.

Perhaps the most touching scene is when the brothers come to the conclusion that God is punishing them because of the way they treated Joseph (verse 21). They still feel guilt over what they did. Joseph is now able to see their remorse. This touched him—so much so that "he turned away from them and began to weep" (verse 24). Joseph's childhood wound is beginning to heal.

When a wound begins to heal, it hurts. That's what happens when the treatment is applied. This is true for physical wounds; but it's also true for emotional ones. God the Great Physician is treating Joseph's wound.

1. Have you ever had déjà vu? How is your experience similar to what happened to Joseph in this chapter?

...And there was light.

2. What emotions do you think Joseph felt when he first saw his brothers? Have you ever felt similar emotions? If so, when?

3. Have you ever had to face something in your past that was painful? If not, do you have anything that needs to be healed?

A Grief Observed

Genesis 43

Then he looked up and saw his brother Benjamin, his mother's son, and said, "Is this your youngest brother, of whom you spoke to me? God be gracious to you, my son!" With that, Joseph hurried out, because he was overcome with affection for his brother, and he was about to weep. So he went into a private room and wept there. Then he washed his face and came out; and controlling himself he said,

And God said…

"Serve the meal." They served him by himself, and them by themselves, and the Egyptians who ate with him by themselves, because the Egyptians could not eat with the Hebrews, for that is an abomination to the Egyptians. (Genesis 43:29-32, NRSV)

You've probably noticed this when you've gotten hurt: the greater the wound, the longer it takes to heal. When you scrape your knee, it takes only a few days. When you break your leg, it takes a few months. It's hard to measure a wound that happens in the heart. These chapters show that a heart wound takes some time to heal.

In the last chapter, Joseph began to feel the emotions of his past. In this chapter, those emotions escalate when his brothers return. Part of the reason is that they bring Benjamin with them. Benjamin is Joseph's only full brother; and with Rachel's death occurring shortly after Benjamin's birth, I'm sure that the two brothers shared a unique bond. This is evident by Joseph's reaction to seeing him. (verse 30). Once more, Joseph weeps, showing again that tears are a part of his healing. Perhaps they're the water God uses to wash our wounds.

If you live anywhere near the ocean, you know that when you go swimming with a scrape, it hurts when you first get in.  … "Let there be light"; …

However, a doctor will tell you that it's a "good hurt," because salt water is good for the wound.

Somehow salt water was good for Joseph's wound too. The more he wept, the softer his heart became, and this was evident in the fact that he serves his brothers a great feast. Although he is not ready to sit with them, he wants to bless them. Joseph's generosity shows the beginning of grace.

Grace begins when we soften our heart and allow God to heal us. Joseph's tears had begun melting the resentment he had stored inside his heart. But it was a process. Many years of suffering had passed since his brothers sold him as a slave. Yet, God had led him through that suffering to the person he'd become. Joseph was probably thinking about all this as his brothers sat to eat.

The chapter ends with Joseph sitting alone—not at his usual place with the Egyptians but not with his brothers either. He is moving toward them, but he's not yet with them. Forgiveness takes time and can happen only when we're ready. And Joseph is on his way there.

1. When you treat a wound and it hurts, is that a good sign or a bad sign? Why?

...And there was light.

2. How are emotional wounds similar to physical wounds? How are they different?

3. Do you think that God wants to heal all of our emotional wounds? Do you have any emotional wounds that God wants to heal?

The Final Payback

Genesis 44

He searched, beginning with the eldest and ending with the youngest; and the cup was found in Benjamin's sack. At this they tore their clothes. Then each one loaded his donkey, and they returned to the city.

Judah and his brothers came to Joseph's house while he was still there; and they fell to the ground before him.
(Genesis 44:12-14, NRSV)

And God said...

It's hard to figure out exactly what motivates Joseph in this chapter. But it's clear that he's still acting from his pain. While the last chapter seemed to end with the hope of forgiveness, this chapter begins with Joseph playing games. He wasn't yet ready for God to break all the way through.

Sometimes when we're about to forgive, we get in touch with some deep hurt that stops us. We feel as though we have to hold on to our pain. Somehow, letting go feels as though we are giving in to the person who has hurt us. So we hold on to our anger as a way of paying that person back. The problem is, we're the ones who suffer from our anger.

Joseph continues toying with his brothers by planting silver in Benjamin's sack, then sending a servant to bring the

person who "stole his silver" back. It was a cruel trick to play, since his brothers couldn't return to their father without Benjamin. But Joseph was not finished punishing them for the past.

Joseph's brothers must have felt like pawns in a chess  **... "Let there be light"; ...** game. They kept being punished for crimes they didn't commit. But what they were really being punished for was what they did to Joseph long ago. And this was Joseph's final act of revenge.

What happens next is a great confession from Joseph's brothers, and it comes from their innocence and fear. Judah pleads with Joseph, telling him they cannot return without

Benjamin. The reason they can't is because Benjamin's brother was lost. It's a heart wrenching plea; and one that succeeded in finally melting Joseph's heart. But the details of Judah's story must have touched Joseph most.

When Judah mentions that Jacob still grieves for Joseph (verse 28), I can only imagine how Joseph felt. The fact that Joseph was gone for so long, yet not forgotten, must have reached deep inside his heart. Judah pleads with Joseph that they cannot return without Benjamin because of the misery that would come upon their father.

That's the line that finally breaks through to Joseph. The next chapter will show how he responds.

1. What was Joseph's final payback in this chapter? What do you think motivated him?

...And there was light.

2. Have you ever "paid someone back" for something he or she did? If not, have you ever wanted to? When?

3. Why do you think it took Joseph so long to forgive his brothers? Has anyone done something to you that was hard to forgive? If so, how did you handle it?

Seeing God's Perspective

Genesis 45

Joseph said to his brothers, "I am Joseph. Is my father still alive?"
But his brothers could not answer him, so dismayed were they at
his presence.
Then Joseph said to his brothers, "Come closer to me." And they
came closer. He said, "I am your brother, Joseph, whom you sold
into Egypt. And now do not be distressed, or angry with

And
God
said . . .

yourselves, because you sold me here; for God
sent me before you to preserve life."
(Genesis 45:3-5, NRSV)

Have you ever looked through a microscope? It's amazing to be focused on something so small. When you pull away, you realize how limited your perspective was. But the big picture looks different because you have a better understanding of the details.

That's a little like what happened to Joseph and his brothers in this chapter. The microscope has been taken away. At first, the shock is a bit much for them; they are terrified at what they now see. But Joseph walks them through the past from God's perspective, and their vision is expanded even further.

In this chapter, we see Joseph's character finally emerge as he reframes the past with God's grace. For three chapters, Joseph has acted out his childhood hurt and anger. Now Joseph is able to see

things from God's perspective, because his painful memories have all been released. His speech is the evidence of his healing, and his words are filled with freedom and grace.

The comfort Joseph imparts to his brothers makes up

. . . **"Let**
there be
light"; . . .

for the grief he has caused them to endure. They've had plenty of opportunity to face the sins of their past. Now they can receive forgiveness so that they can move on. Joseph not only extends this forgiveness, he reinterprets their actions as good—in light of the bigger picture. This shows the maturity of Joseph's faith.

We finally see how Joseph's trials have contributed to the

man he has become. Joseph has been tested and tried; and he has emerged victorious. The words he speaks to his brothers in this chapter are a far cry from the words he spoke to them years ago. At that time, he was a proud and haughty little brother. Now he is a mature man of God. His tears show his humility, while his words show his wisdom and strength.

Not only was this scene tremendously healing for Joseph's brothers, it was a witness to all who heard it from afar. When grace spills over from our hearts, it touches everyone around us. Joseph's journey has enough grace to touch us all.

...And there was light.

1. How did Joseph reinterpret his past in this chapter? How do you think it made his brothers feel?

2. Have you ever looked back on something with a different perspective than when you were experiencing it? If so, how was it different?

3. Has something bad ever happened to you that God used for good? What does that tell you about God?

Jacob's Final Promise

Genesis 46

God spoke to Israel in visions of the night, and said, "Jacob, Jacob." And he said, "Here I am." Then he said, "I am God, the God of your father; do not be afraid to go down to Egypt, for I will make of you a great nation there. I myself will go down with you to Egypt, and I will also bring you up again; and Joseph's own hand shall close your eyes."

And God said ... (Genesis 46:2-4, NRSV)

One of the greatest powers God holds is the power of redemption, and God uses it to redeem us. But God is also able to redeem our stories. In this chapter, we see how Jacob's story is redeemed.

When Jacob first found out that Joseph was gone, he cried "In mourning will I go down to the grave to my son" (37:35, NIV). But God steps in to reveal a different ending to Jacob's story. And Jacob had to believe God for the new ending to unfold.

Jacob is told that if he goes to Egypt with his family, he will die with Joseph closing his eyes. It must have been difficult for Jacob to believe, since he'd lived his own story of grief for many years. But Jacob had to let go of that story in order to live God's story. And at some point, we need to do that too.

Sometimes we end up living stories of hopelessness and despair, because of our lack of vision. This was certainly true of Jacob. He had been living his story based on what he could see, but God rewrote Jacob's story to include things he  ... **"Let there be light"; ...** couldn't see. Jacob had to let go of his story to live the new story God had planned.

Believe it or not, some people are unable to let go of their stories. They end up stuck in their hopelessness and despair. Somehow believing that something good can happen is too scary, so they live with the familiarity of their pain. Jacob could have done that, and he would have missed all that God had in store. He also would have missed seeing God's story come to pass. Instead, Jacob let go of his old life and followed God. This made way for all that God was going to do.

Jacob's story was part of a bigger story that God was creating, but Jacob had to live his own story first. Jacob gathered his family and moved to Egypt to be with Joseph. But he also began an important chapter in Israel's life.

One day the Israelites would leave Egypt, but Jacob would be long since gone. His role was to get the Israelites *to* Egypt, and he did it by following God to his son.

1. If Jacob hadn't listened to God and gone to Egypt, how would his life have turned out? Would it have been better or worse?

...And there was light.

2. How does this chapter show that God has good plans for our life? Is there an area of your life where you need that hope?

3. How was Jacob's story part of a bigger story that God was weaving for the Israelites? What does that tell you about the way God works in our lives?

Authority From God

Genesis 47

Then Joseph brought in his father Jacob, and presented him before Pharaoh, and Jacob blessed Pharaoh. Pharaoh said to Jacob, "How many are the years of your life?" Jacob said to Pharaoh, "The years of my earthly sojourn are one hundred thirty; few and hard have been the years of my life. They do not compare with the years of the life of my ancestors during their long sojourn." Then Jacob blessed Pharaoh, and went out from the presence of Pharaoh. (Genesis 47:7-10, NRSV)

And God said...

Pharaoh was the person who held the highest authority in Egypt. Some people regarded him as a god. Even Joseph, with all his might and majesty, was subject to him. That's what makes the events of this chapter so intriguing.

Jacob has come with his family to Egypt to be reunited with Joseph. The meeting between them is tender and tearful, and there is a great sense of completion now that the family is together. Egypt will be their new home, so Joseph must ask Pharaoh's permission to reside in his land.

Pharaoh immediately gives Joseph's family permission to settle in one of the best territories in Egypt. But it's what happens next that stands out as a surprise. Joseph presents his father to Pharaoh, and verse seven says, "Jacob blessed Pharaoh." Can you imagine what that was like? Here was the most powerful figure in all of Egypt, being "blessed" by an old Hebrew patriarch. I'm sure that there was a moment where Joseph flinched, embarrassed by his dad's actions.

... "Let there be light"; ...

But the amazing thing was Pharaoh's response: "How old are you?" Pharaoh asked Jacob. Joseph must have breathed a sigh of relief. Perhaps Pharaoh would understand that his father was aged and senile, and excuse him for being presumptuous. But Jacob stood confident, knowing that he had an authority beyond Pharaoh.

Instead of giving his age, Jacob proclaims that the years of his sojourn are a small part of the pilgrimage his ancestors have made. By answering this way, Jacob establishes his authority as part of a chosen chain of God. Pharaoh might have the authority of man, but Jacob has the authority of God. That is why Jacob blesses Pharaoh.

The picture of this old Hebrew man blessing this powerful king is one worth pondering. I can only imagine how it looked. But at that moment, Jacob established his authority as different from Pharaoh, and Pharaoh accepted the blessing with grace.

It's a small glimpse into the difference between earthly power and heavenly power. And it sets the tone for the coming king—a king whose authority would come from Heaven. But instead of a throne, he would preside from a cross.

1. How do you think Pharaoh felt when Jacob blessed him? How do you think Joseph felt?

...And there was light.

2. What was the difference between Pharaoh's authority and Jacob's authority? Who was greater? Why?

3. How is earthly power different from heavenly power? Which is more important? Which would you rather have?

History Repeats Itself

When Israel saw Joseph's sons, he said, "Who are these?" Joseph said to his father, "They are my sons, whom God has given me here." And he said, "Bring them to me, please, that I may bless them...."

And God said...

But Israel stretched out his right hand and laid it on the head of Ephraim, who was the younger, and his left hand on the head of Manasseh, crossing his hands, for Manasseh was the firstborn.
(Genesis 48:8-9, 14, NRSV)

Of all the events of Jacob's life, this chapter contains the one he is remembered for most. Hebrews 11:21 chooses this scene as the best demonstration of Jacob's faith. A closer look shows us why.

Joseph is told to bring his sons to Jacob so that he can bless them. When Jacob starts to bless Ephraim, Joseph's second son, Joseph gently corrects him by moving his hand to Manasseh's head. Manasseh, being the eldest, was supposed to be first. But Jacob knows exactly what he is doing. Ephraim, although he is second born, will be ahead of Manasseh. Jacob is called to repeat his own history by blessing the second son.

In some ways, it's a scene that directly mirrors Jacob's past. However, there are distinct differences that show how

Jacob has matured. Perhaps that is why this is the scene Jacob is remembered for most.

When Jacob received *his* blessing, it came with the price of manipulation and deceit. He had been prophe-sied to receive the blessing; however, instead of waiting for it, he

..."Let there be light";...

tricked Esau and Isaac to obtain it. Jacob got his blessing, but the process was less than admirable (see Genesis 27).

In this chapter, Jacob displays a calm trust as he fulfills a similar prophecy. Ephraim is to be ahead of Manasseh, and Jacob's gentle demeanor and calm words to Joseph (verse 19) show how confident he is in the timing and fulfillment of his task.

It's as if God gives Jacob a chance to redo his past, and he does it when he blesses these two sons. For this reason, Jacob is not remembered in the Faith Hall of Fame (Hebrews 11) for his own blessing. Instead, he is remembered for blessing Joseph's sons.

It's a testimony that God gives us chances to do things over. And what God remembers is when we get it right.

1. How was the blessing of Ephraim and Manasseh similar to that of Jacob and Esau? How was it different?

...And there was light.

2. What changes do you observe in Jacob now that he is an older man? What evidence do you see that he trusts God more?

3. How does this chapter show God's desire to help us grow? What might God be trying to teach you? How would you be different if you were the person God wanted you to be?

A Shadow of Things to Come

Genesis 49

Assemble and hear, O sons of Jacob;
listen to Israel your father....
Judah, your brothers shall praise you;
your hand shall be on the neck of your enemies;
your father's sons shall bow down before you....
The scepter shall not depart from Judah,

And

God

said ...

nor the ruler's staff from between his feet,
until tribute comes to him;
and the obedience of the peoples is his.
(Genesis 49:2, 8, 10, NRSV)

In this chapter, we get our first glimpse of Jesus. It comes from a dying man's words. Genesis 2 briefly alluded to the day when the serpent would be crushed by Eve's offspring. But this chapter reveals the origin of the "offspring." Jacob's words to Judah are that "the scepter will not depart from Judah" (verse 10). So we learn that Judah's line will bring us our king.

It's a bit puzzling that the fourth son of Jacob would carry this honor. But as the chapter unfolds, we see why. Reuben, the eldest son, seems the logical choice. But Reuben has defiled his father's bed. By sleeping with Bilhah (35:22), he has lost his father's honor. Because of that, Reuben no longer excels. Simeon and Levi are next in line for Jacob's blessing. But Genesis 34 tells of

their darkened past. Thus, Jacob curses their anger (verse 7), and he tells them that their descendants will be dispersed.

So Judah is chosen. Jacob says that the "ruler's staff" will eventually be his. It is a prophecy that holds the promise of  ... "Let there be light"; ...
kingship, and there are two ways that this prophecy will come to pass: Initially, it will be fulfilled in the coming of David. But ultimately, it will be fulfilled in Jesus Christ. One will be an earthly king; the other, a heavenly one. But the heavenly king will be the greatest king of all.

Jacob goes on to bless his other sons; and his words are for them and their descendants.

Jacob's sons will become the twelve tribes of Israel, and this chapter reveals how these tribes began. As we've seen before in Genesis, God's plan works in concert with our choices. Jacob's prophecy shows a combination of both. There were consequences and rewards for each son for his behavior, but there was also the presence of grace.

Grace is found in the fourth son's blessing. He was given the kingdom because he was next in line. It's the first glimpse that God's kingdom cannot be earned, but simply given. And Judah experienced this grace first.

1. Why, do you think, was Judah chosen to carry the seed of the future king? Was it because he was greater than his brothers? Why, why not?

...And there was light.

2. How does Jacob's blessing to his sons show that God rewards faithfulness? How does it show God's grace?

3. How is the way Judah received God's kingdom similar to the way we receive God's kingdom? Is there anything we have to do to receive it? Why, or why not?

God's Purpose Revealed

Realizing that their father was dead, Joseph's brothers said, "What if Joseph still bears a grudge against us and pays us back in full for all the wrong that we did to him?" ...

Then his brothers also wept, fell down before him, and said, "We are here as your slaves." But Joseph said to them, "Do not be

And God said ...

afraid! Am I in the place of God? Even though you intended to do harm to me, God intended it for good, in order to preserve a numerous people, as he is doing today."

(Genesis 50:15, 18-20, NRSV)

There is only one way to see all that God has done in our lives. It happens as we look back. By looking in the rearview mirror of our lives, we see clearly what is behind us. That's what Joseph does in this chapter.

Throughout Genesis, we've traveled with many people on their journey, and we've learned important lessons from each of their lives. Now in this final chapter, we look back, through the eyes of Joseph, and the grand scope of God's purpose is revealed.

After Jacob dies, Joseph fulfills his vow to have him buried with Abraham and Isaac. His brothers go with him to complete the task. After they bury their father, Joseph's brothers are afraid that Joseph will turn on them. But Joseph's words reflect the healing that has taken place. Not only has

Joseph totally forgiven them, he is able to reinterpret their actions as part of God's will. It is the definition of amazing grace.

As we've learned from each life we've studied, suffering is part of the journey. However, it's not a part that we easily embrace.

... "Let there be light"; ...

In spite of that, God allows pain to do its work in us. When we look in the rearview mirror, we see what our pain has produced.

For Joseph, the pain included being unfairly scorned by his brothers and wrongfully accused by Potiphar's wife. He went from living as a slave to sitting forgotten as a prisoner. For two years, Joseph served an unjust sentence in a prison